Embedding organisational learning for
high performance using the MILL model

A Practical Guide for
BEHAVIOURAL
LEADERSHIP

Arjan Molenkamp

First published in 2018 by Grammar Factory Pty Ltd.

All enquiries should be made to the author on info@managementmastermind.com
or at www.managementmastermind.com

ISBN: 978-0-6481371-9-1 (paperback)
ISBN: 978-0-6481372-1-4 (hardback)
ISBN: 978-0-6481372-0-7 (eBook)

Printed by IngramSpark & Lightning Source®

Cover design by Designerbility

Editing and book production by Grammar Factory

Disclaimer

The material in this publication is of the nature of general comment only, and does not
represent professional advice. It is not intended to provide specific guidance for particular
circumstances and it should not be relied on as the basis for any decision to take action or
not take action on any matter which it covers. Readers should obtain professional advice
where appropriate, before making any such decision. To the maximum extent permitted by
law, the author and publisher disclaim all responsibility and liability to any person, arising
directly or indirectly from any person taking or not taking action based on the information
in this publication.

For Ryan

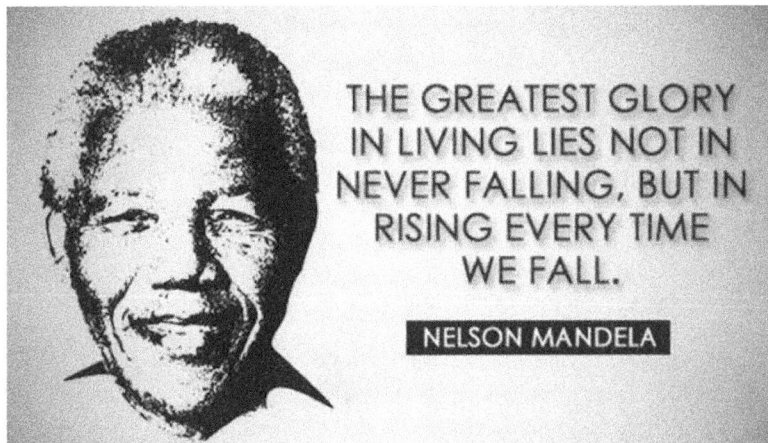

THE GREATEST GLORY
IN LIVING LIES NOT IN
NEVER FALLING, BUT IN
RISING EVERY TIME
WE FALL.

NELSON MANDELA

CONTENTS

TURNING THREATS INTO OPPORTUNITIES

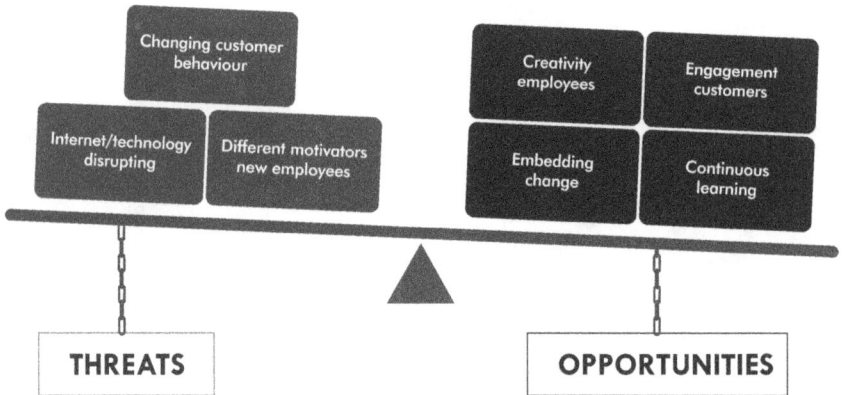

Changing customer behaviour		Creativity employees	Engagement customers
Internet/technology disrupting	Different motivators new employees	Embedding change	Continuous learning

THREATS

The Internet has made markets transparent and gave customers global access to products and services. Expectations are higher and poor service is immediately escalated to a broad audience before management is even aware. The new generation of employees wants to be more involved and engaged.

OPPORTUNITIES

Teaming up with customers and employees by organising more structured engagement will result in continuous learning and improvement. Both customers and employees know what they want and what can be done. Interactive learning leadership will guide this process of becoming best in class.

MANAGEMENT
MASTER MIND

INTRODUCTION

'We are what we repeatedly do.
Excellence, then, is not an act, but a habit.'

ARISTOTLE

All businesses today are feeling the impact of the digitisation of the modern world. In just a few decades, developments such as the internet and social media have changed our lives in ways we never imagined. New technologies, such as augmented reality and 3D-printing, are beginning to have an impact that we cannot predict, and who knows what brave new technological revolution is just over the horizon. This development shows no signs of slowing down and it has created, and will continue to create, new and unforeseen challenges for businesses, as it hardly seems possible to have a roadmap for navigating and adapting to a faster and faster rate of change.

In this climate of faster and faster change, there will inevitably be new entrants to the market and significant changes to customer behaviour. Some organisations consider these events to be serious challenges. Other companies view digital developments and their impact on the business landscape to be tremendous opportunities because they provide a chance to reduce costs and expand access to new markets. In both instances, the need to respond at a faster pace is increasing. There are challenges, however, in terms of how to respond.

- Organisations have always been forced to create new developments as a result of changes in market and customer behaviour. The difference is that **these days the changes are much more disruptive; that is, they are revolutionary changes rather than evolutionary ones.** Digital challenges are ongoing and it is not always clear which developments are relevant and which ones are not. This poses significant strategic questions for organisations in terms of whether to act and try to lead, or wait a while, react, and then follow.

- The new generation of employees has different expectations on how the interaction with management should take place. They have grown up with internet and social media and they are used to engaging with the whole world, knowing what is going on and spreading their opinion to a wide network. They also expect the same kind of involvement, transparency and engagement in their working environment. They feel that having fun with the team and meaningful work is more important than money and career. They are well educated and have lots of ideas. **Management should nourish these qualities of the new generation by sharing more on strategy and purpose, but also by engaging staff more in innovation and development.**

- Customers have high expectations, and because it is easy to globally access products and services, they are unlikely to remain loyal to a particular brand or provider. **Because developments these days move at a much faster rate, this could create a gap that cannot be bridged if organisations take too long to respond.** This could result in a decline in market shares. Reacting to new developments with a 'me too' strategy (i.e. copying and pasting ideas from competitors) will never be enough to attract new customers and may, over time, result in a loss of customers. The need to respond faster and to differentiate more is growing, but it is difficult to make accurate business decisions in such turbulent environments.

These challenges have already resulted in the development of new organisational structures and work processes like Agile and Lean. The Information and Communications Technology (ICT) sector has the leading edge in this modern style of working and some of these principles are also being applied to other sectors.

> **The key principles that need to be applied in order to respond to the changing environment are basically the same: flexibility and action learning.**

Something needs to change, but it is risky to make decisions that are set in stone. Developments progress quickly and there is always a risk of 'betting on the wrong horse'. There is, therefore, a need for an ongoing process to 'try and learn', which requires a different approach in management and employee engagement.

This book describes how to act/react within our ever-changing digital world. A new model called the **Molenkamp Interactive Learning Leadership (MILL) model** will be presented. It describes how innovation and learning leadership can be implemented at any level within any organisation.

WHY THIS BOOK IS DIFFERENT

There are many models on management and leadership, all of which try to explain a piece of the puzzle. Studying those models can be very inspiring, as they provide ideas about what can be done, but implementation of the models is generally still hard. This is because most models do not include an end-to-end description of how the theory of the model has to be implemented in the daily routine. Even if there is such a practical guideline, the impact will still be limited due to the model's limited scope.

The MILL model is different. It is a ready-to-implement approach for building a **Learning High Performing Organisation (LHPO)**. This book gives a complete toolbox and covers the most important principles and methodologies for setting up an LHPO. The starting point for developing the model was the aspiration to offer a total solution for any organisation that has ambitions to get the best out of their employees. The model has also been developed and structured to both show the big picture – an overview on a high level – and allow zooming in on the detail in order to understand the implementation challenges and opportunities.

Management is more of an art than a science, and books that claim they have researched and found the magic formula for business success are merely showing some correlation between success and management style or between stock price and innovation budget but there is no magic formula. However, there are various techniques, a wealth of knowledge and a vast amount of experience which, if applied well, can make a big difference. This will all be shared throughout the book. Recommendations made in this book stem from personal experiences and insights gained from reading many books and articles on management. This book is also based upon concepts that have been practised, and improved, with convincing results in various countries and in different scenarios, from mergers to sales campaigns.

The MILL model combines some existing concepts and ideas with new insights and best practices. Within the model, there is a strong focus on connecting the various concepts to ensure that they can be used simultaneously and mutually reinforce each other.

The MILL model is also aimed at giving guidance on how management can align their leadership style with the changing business environment. The internet is disrupting businesses, which requires a more experimental and innovative leadership style.

> *Organisations are expected to be able to respond quicker to this changing environment, and the required change is more drastic and therefore harder.*

Rapid and drastic change can only be achieved with a high level of staff empowerment and staff buy-in. While these changes are happening in the environment, the staff composition is also changing and a new generation is entering organisations. This new generation is highly educated, but also has high expectations in terms of being involved, challenged and groomed. The new generation is even more interested in being engaged and challenged in their work than in rewards and status. The MILL model has therefore also been developed as a model for increased staff empowerment in order to explore the potential of the new generation of workers. These youngsters have been raised in the digital age and are likely to have more and better ideas than the older generation of managers.

The MILL model is aimed at implementing interactive learning leadership for organisations that want to become a high-performance organisation. Interactive means that a lot of engagement is expected between management and employees, and that there will be two-way communication instead of only top-down communication. The interaction is focused on learning, and the philosophy is that:

> *Successes can be used to learn what works well and failures can be used to learn what can be improved.*

In other words, whatever the outcome, something can be learned and be used to make the organisation grow.

HOW TO USE THIS BOOK

Part 1 and 2 aim at creating a broad understanding of the entire model, like a roadmap that shows where you are and where you are going. First, an overview of the MILL model is provided. Next, the four blades of the model are introduced. Then we look at the guiding principles and key tools that are required in order to guide the implementation of the model – in other words, how the blades of the model are connected. Parts 3–6 expand on this introduction and look in more detail at each building block of the four blades. They describe the steps, structures and processes for implementation. If you lose sight of the bigger picture while proceeding in more detail in this section, you can still go back and check how a topic fits the MILL model by referring to the overview in Part 1. Part 7 discusses what is required in order for existing management structures to be able to accommodate the new approach. Implementing change will always be challenging and there are pitfalls along the way, so Part 7 shares some tools and techniques that can be used to overcome these when embedding the MILL model in any organisation.

The way the book is structured aims at maximising its practical usage by keeping things simple. This means that most topics only cover the four most relevant variations. There may be 100 ways to provide feedback and perhaps 100 options for, say, action improvement, but for the sake of simplicity either a selection of the four most relevant examples is used or a multiple of options are clustered into four groups. Every chapter is written in such a way that it can be read without reference to other chapters.

Nevertheless, for an improved understanding and a more successful implementation, it is recommended that readers follow the sequence – from Part 1 through Part 7.

This book is neither about providing quick fixes nor is it a project to be completed within a certain period in order to build an LHPO. Utilising the approaches explained in this book to strengthen an organisational structure and culture are not complicated, but they will take time. The book contains some quick wins that help organisations begin the process of making improvements, but a consistent effort is required to stay at the highest possible performance levels.

> *It is not true that 'knowledge is power', but rather that 'acting on knowledge is power'.*

Each chapter requires some sort of action in terms of its translation, application and evaluation of the insights it imparts. It is recommended that all of the suggested practices are implemented, even if some of them may have been tried before and found to be a failure. When the MILL model is applied in its entirety, a different and better result can be expected.

> *All elements of the MILL model are interconnected in some way, and by working your way through each one, the best possible outcome will be achieved.*

Enjoy the ride and have fun celebrating the success this book will help you to create!

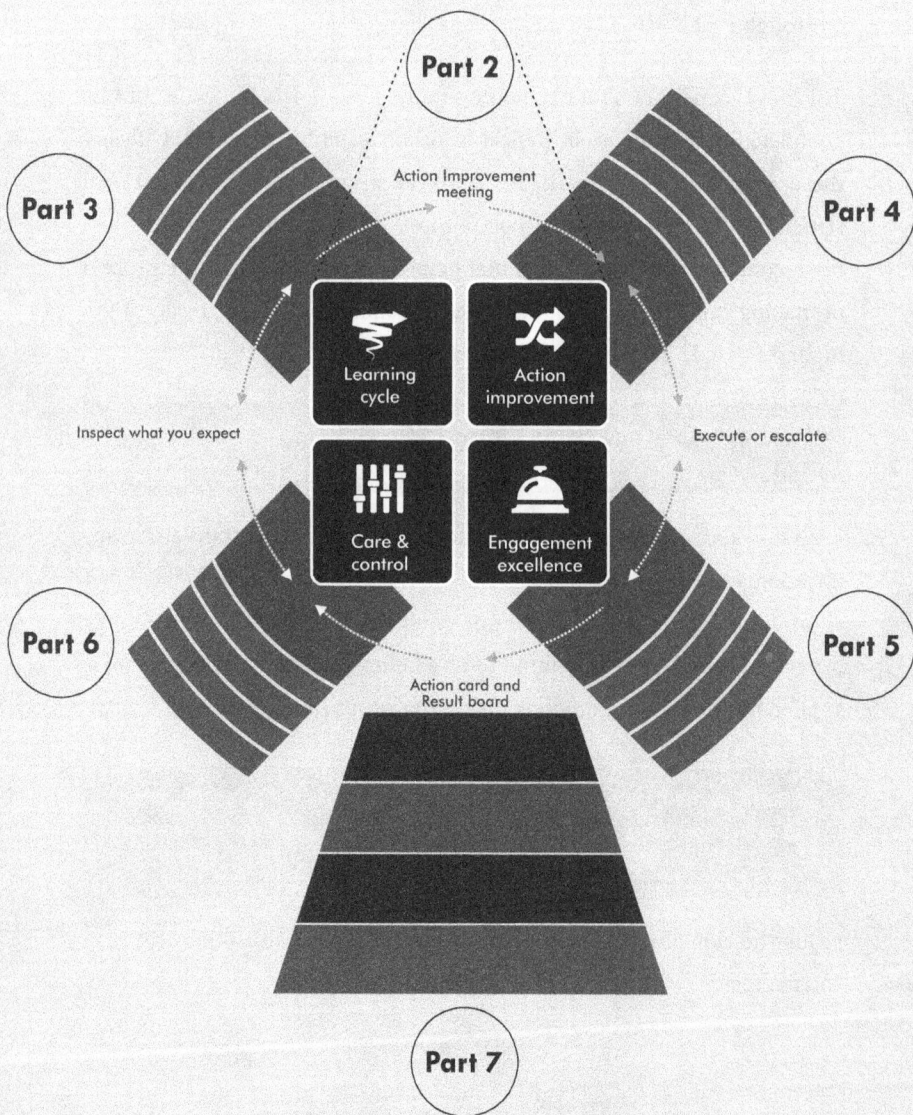

Part 2

Action Improvement
meeting

Part 3

Part 4

Learning
cycle

Action
improvement

Inspect what you expect

Execute or escalate

Care &
control

Engagement
excellence

Part 6

Part 5

Action card and
Result board

Part 7

PART 1:
THE MILL MODEL

The first part of this book will give you a high-level overview of the MILL model. The graph may look a bit overwhelming, but understanding how the various parts of this book are interconnected will make it easier to dig deeper into these parts. The key messages for the book are as follows:

- Part 3: The manager should be able to organise a learning-by-doing environment to get the best out of employees and teams.

- Part 4: The employees should be able to identify areas for improvement and understand what kind of change is required to develop new skills and competencies.

- Part 5: The employee can learn most during daily engagements if there is a structured approach aiming for receiving feedback on every step in the process.

- Part 6: The manager has to follow up and give feedback and show care and control to support and stretch employees for continuous learning and increasing results.

- To connect and support these parts, there are still two additional parts that are required to make the whole model work properly and sustainable:

- Part 2: The parts 3 to 6, also called the blades, will be connected by guiding tools and key principles as described in this part

- Part 7: This part will describe four organisational requirements that should be in place as foundation for a successful implementation of the MILL model.

OVERVIEW OF THE MILL MODEL

The manager initiates the **learning cycle** by seeking commitment from employees on **action improvement.** Commitments will then be executed using the **engagement excellence** approach, during which time the manager will stay involved by showing **care and control.**

Applying the MILL model will facilitate organisational learning that will result in higher performance.

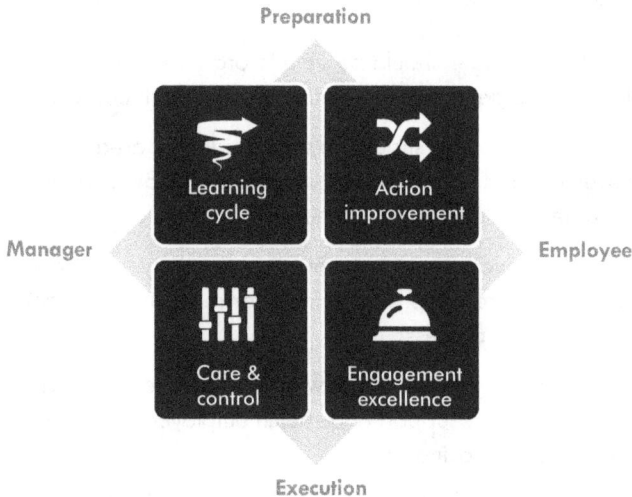

Preparation

Manager

Employee

Learning cycle

Action improvement

Care & control

Engagement excellence

Execution

In traditional management, the manager is more focussed on preparation and the employee is primarily involved in execution. The MILL model does not have such a split, as both managers and employees have a role to play in execution and preparation.

The outcome of using the MILL model is more empowerment and more impact for better results!

MANAGEMENT MASTER MIND

CHAPTER 1

OVERVIEW OF THE MILL MODEL

'Yesterday is gone. Tomorrow has not yet come.
We have only today.
Let us begin.'

MOTHER TERESA (ATTRIBUTED)

The MILL model is constructed of four sectors, or **'blades'**, that work together to help an organisation become a **Learning High Performing Organisation (LHPO).** Each blade is constructed of several building blocks, which make up the day-to-day focus for an organisation. The four blades are connected by a set of **key tools** and **guiding principles** that ensure that the entire mechanism works together. Let's take a look at each of these components.

- The first blade of the MILL model is the **learning cycle** and explains the role of managers in guiding the whole learning process for both the employees and themselves. The manager is the overall owner of the learning cycle and facilitates the process. Stretching employees and getting clear **commitment** from them will be followed up by improved **actions** with a focus on **delivery.** The manager has to support and stimulate the process of learning from both successes and failures, and those lessons provide input for another round of improvement in the next learning cycle.

- The second blade is called **action improvement**, and describes what is expected from employees in terms of coming up with ideas for action improvements (behavioural change). Employees' ideas should be based on what they have learned so far or what they want to explore to see whether it works. These ideas can be grouped in categories related to quantity of work (**more** work) and quality of work (**better** work). To find the time for stretching and to explore other opportunities, staff will also be challenged to see what can be done in two more categories: doing things **differently** (creativity) or doing things **less** (efficiency).

- **Engagement excellence** is the third blade of the model and describes how the first two blades can be used for daily engagements and what specific steps are required to learn and improve after each engagement. Employees are guided how to structure engagement with their stakeholders (customers, colleagues or others) in such a way that best results will be achieved and best input for learning will be collected. The focus during these engagements is on customer needs, followed by managing expectations and checking whether **needs** are well understood. **Execution** will be aligned with these needs and **expectations**, and afterwards there will be an assessment of the overall **experience** as input for learning and improvement.

- The last blade of the MILL model is **care and control**. This will explain that the role of the manager is to stay involved and get the best out of both the individual employees and the team. The manager has a duty to show daily care and control towards employees in order to support and stretch them for continuous learning. Driving results and grooming employees goes hand-in-hand with identifying the strengths and weaknesses of individuals, as well as exploring organisational opportunities for further improvement. An employee's progress and the impact of their work are used for **analysis** and **feedback** to help them fulfil their potential, which is in the best interest of all stakeholders.

The four blades of the MILL model are connected by a set of key tools and guiding principles. With the support of these tools and principles, the blades can mutually reinforce each other.

- The first tool is the **action improvement meeting (AIM)** and connects the learning cycle with action improvement. The process of turning employees' ideas for action improvement into firm commitments will be done during these meetings. During the meeting it will be made clear what the actions will look like, but also what results are expected. The action improvement meeting takes place on a weekly basis and requires the involvement of all team members under the guidance of the manager.

- **Execute or escalate** is the guiding principle that connects action improvement with engagement excellence and is a primary focus for employees. This principle is introduced to make sure that employees are serious about their commitments. The manager is not supposed to waste time by micro-managing employees and checking whether they stick to their commitment. Employees have a duty to let the manager know if there is any reason for not sticking to their action improvement commitment when executing engagement excellence.

- The **action card** and **result board** are key tools that work together to connect engagement excellence to care and control. During the week, employees are required to track activities and achievements to measure progress and do some analysis on what worked well and what did not work well. This kind of tracking also helps the manager to have meaningful interventions with their employees. The manager is supposed to guide the learning process, and therefore has to see how effort and impact differ between employees.

- The principle of **inspect what you expect** connects the learning cycle with care and control and is the focus for management. While the execute or escalate principle provides employees with their own link between preparation and execution, the manager also has to show that he or she is serious by applying care and control when implementing the learning cycle. The manager's principle is called 'inspect what you expect' and it urges managers to 'put their money where their mouth is' by being involved and showing care for what they claim is important.

In the next chapter we will look in more detail at the building blocks of each blade of the model, which will be fully unpacked and discussed in Parts 3–6. It is important to understand the whole model before zooming in on the blades, and thereafter zooming in further on the building blocks of the blades. Once the bigger picture is understood, then zooming in will provide examples on how to make the model work.

THE LEARNING CYCLE
(MANAGER/PREPARATION)

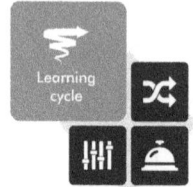

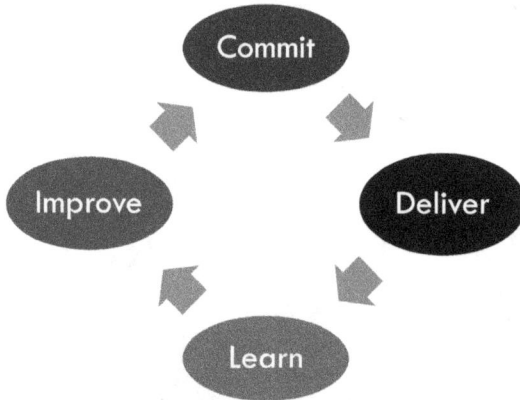

The learning cycle requires strong upfront commitment from employees on action goals and result goals; strong focus is required to achieve the best results. The MILL model aims for a tangible outcome, hence the focus on delivery. Both results and lessons learned are acceptable deliverables. Understanding what worked and what did not work is both considered to be a successful outcome of engagement to continue the learning cycle.

Learning is about measuring and understanding how outcome is related to effort. This will give a better insight of how impact was created and what are the root causes of failures. These learnings will be used by employees as input for the development of new ideas for further improvement.

The best ideas are selected and made more specific before the cycle starts afresh by creating new commitment for another learning cycle.

CHAPTER 2:

THE LEARNING CYCLE

'Excellent firms do not believe in excellence,
only in constant improvement and constant change.'

TOM PETERS

The first blade of the MILL model is the **learning cycle**. The universal principle of a learning cycle has been described by many authors in the past, but also in more modern methodologies like 'Scrum' or 'Agile'. The principles of these approaches are similar in that the goal is always the same – learning by doing. This is also called action learning.

Action learning is based on real life situations rather than theoretical examples taught in a classroom setting. Learning by doing has advantages over traditional learning and results in faster and more intense learning. Action learning can also be more rewarding and fun. Feedback is received directly from the recipient/beneficiary rather than a teacher/trainer, and the results are real and therefore more compelling than simply getting a good score on a paper. Action learning is done as a team effort under the MILL model; by challenging and supporting each other, team members will not only learn from each other, but also celebrate successes as a team.

This chapter will introduce you to the four steps in the learning cycle. Learning cycles are created by breaking bigger assignments down into smaller segments. This allows smaller steps to be taken for faster and easier learning and improvement. As we learn new activities, such as football, mathematics and even dating, we learn by trial and error. By keeping the trials small, the 'errors' feel unimportant, but it's these 'failures' that create the most powerful learnings.

It's important to understand that:

> *You always learn a lot more when you lose than when you win.*

There should be a reflection, at least once a week, on successes and failures, and on corrections and lessons learned. This makes it possible to adjust the on-the-go action. When implementing the learning cycle in this way, the learning by doing process is speeded up and allows for more flexibility. This is different from the traditional development approach in which a lot of time is spent on extensive analysis in order to come up with a bulky plan – one that is difficult to implement and still has an uncertain outcome. The process described here allows employees to interact more frequently and it is more suited to the disruptive markets that most organisations are facing nowadays.

Now let's look in more detail at the four steps in the learning cycle.

COMMIT

> *The process of learning can only begin if there are strong and clear commitments to improvement.*

Learning requires some change – things must be done differently in order to achieve a better result. Because the effort required will be beyond existing experience and the outcome will be uncertain, some sort of resistance is to be expected. But if these improvements were easy to implement, everybody else would be performing them and no added value would be created. Activities that require the most stretch are also generally the most rewarding because they are likely to raise people to levels that can't easily be reached. But any stretch has to start with a level of commitment, which can also be interpreted as having a will to succeed. Unless there is commitment, from the beginning, to do what needs to be done, you will find yourself a victim of the old adage, 'You can bring the horses to water, but you cannot make them drink'.

> *Commitment goes beyond goal-setting. It includes the attitude and drive required to achieve the final outcome – whatever it takes.*

A goal will give direction, but does not take into account the path towards the end result or what kind of obstacles can be expected along the way. A goal needs reinforcement to overcome these kinds of challenges. By adding a stronger attitude – one that involves a determination to achieve despite challenges, goals will be transformed into commitment. Commitment is the performance spirit required in order to keep moving forward regardless of the obstacles.

> *When there is commitment, obstacles are no longer used as excuses, but are perceived as the hurdles to overcome in order to become stronger.*

DELIVER

This step is about creating an orientation point. When marines are dropped off in unfamiliar territories, their priority is to establish an orientation point before making the next move. If they do not do this, they may get lost. An orientation point helps us to see any progress that needs to be made and which direction to take before the journey begins. By describing in detail the deliverable or expected **outcome**, an orientation point is created that will provide guidance when evaluating whether the employee is on track.

> *You can only find something if you know what you're looking for. A better description of the expected result will create better progress.*

The goal of this step is to come up with something tangible that adds value to the organisation and is in line with the commitment. This can be either a (financial) result or a practical insight (lesson learned), but it must be a tangible outcome of a fully committed effort. For example, it is not good enough simply to call some prospects on a Friday afternoon and, when the phone is not picked up, claim that the new action improvement does not work.

Learning can only take place if it is made clear from the beginning what the expectations are. Creating clarity on the targeted deliverable is the step where those expectations are defined. These expectations will later on be compared with the outcome in order to understand the impact of the effort as input for considering further action improvement. It is important to focus on always bringing back some deliverable – either in terms of results or lessons learned. Results might be as expected, better than expected or below expectations. But as long as valuable lessons are learned when the outcome falls below expectations, the insights gained can be appreciated and therefore the action can still be considered successful.

LEARN

The focus of the MILL model is on creating a learning by doing environment. The third step in the learning cycle is about reviewing how deliverables relate to commitment – in other words:

> **What was the impact of the action?**

Did the impact meet expectations in terms of the expected correlation between effort and results? Was it clear how these results were created, or did the impact fall below expectations? And finally, is there room for improvement? For example, if two employees both committed to call ten prospects, it could be assumed that five would be interested in setting up a meeting. One colleague might manage to set up meetings with six out of the ten prospects called, and the other might only manage to set up three meetings. What caused the difference and what can be improved?

> *The learning cycle guarantees success when it is executed well; either the outcome meets expectations, or valuable lessons are learned when it does not.*

Where expectations were not met, it's important to analyse root causes and understand how and where improvements can be made. This will facilitate the learning process. It is futile to lay blame on circumstances, point fingers at others, or make excuses for under-achievement. Valuable insights can only be translated into improvements when there is a clear understanding of the challenges that lie below the surface, not by simply addressing 'the tip of the iceberg'. Later in the book, symptoms that may indicate where the challenges lie will be described. These symptoms require some further questioning and deeper digging into the root causes to create in-depth learning.

IMPROVE

The final step in completing the learning cycle is to identify specific areas needing improvement.

> **If you continue doing what you have always done, you are likely to achieve similar results.**

Success and growth can be ensured by continuously aiming to do better, more or different than before. For example, a football coach evaluates the performance of the team during the first half and determines what they need to do to improve their performance during the second half. This is discussed with the team at half time and a strategy is agreed to. After the match, if the coach feels there are other ways the team can improve, these are included in the team's training program and practised regularly in preparation for their next match.

> **Reviewing the impact created by employees' efforts and using this knowledge to create action improvements is the essence of the learning cycle.**

After the team effort of identifying how to make improvements, it makes sense to practise the agreed actions among the team to help employees feel more confident with them. Action improvements should also be applied to areas of strength when the results are in line with, or perhaps exceed expectations. This helps employees stay ahead of the curve by further exploring what already works well. It should be made clear that both success and failure qualify for learning, and that:

> *This last step of action improvement does not focus on weaknesses, but on furthering potential and abilities.*

The focus should alternate between becoming even better at what goes well and attempting to improve employees' weaker areas that have potential for growth.

ACTION IMPROVEMENT
(EMPLOYEE/PREPARATION)

Action improvement is the second blade of the MILL model. The focus for action improvement is to make clear what behavioural change can be expected. Depending on the challenges or opportunities an organisation is facing, action improvement can aim to do something more, better, different or less. Actions will be committed to in order to raise the bar for improving quantity, quality, creativity or efficiency.

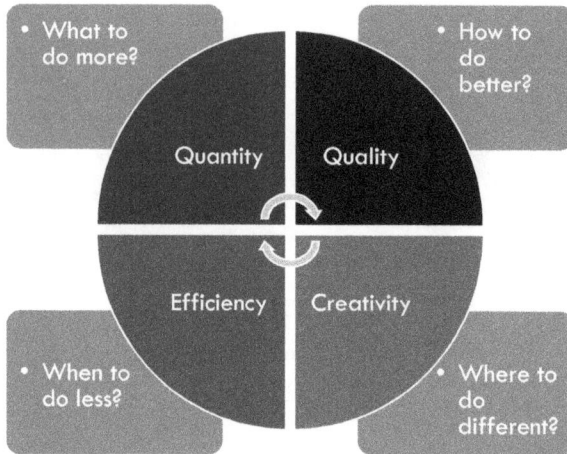

Small steps of continuous action improvement, completed on a weekly basis, can create a big difference in the long run. Challenging a team to take ownership for action improvement creates empowerment, excitement, quicker implementation and better ideas. There is always room for improvement and by alternating between the four options, new ideas can be generated continuously.

MANAGEMENT
MASTER MIND

CHAPTER 3

ACTION IMPROVEMENT

'If you always do what you always did,
you will always get what you always got.'

ALBERT EINSTEIN

The second building block of the MILL model focuses on behavioural changes. First, let's clarify exactly what is meant by 'behavioural' and exactly what needs to change.

> *People generally do not like to be changed, and a manager who pushes an individual to make changes when they are not ready or confident enough to do so may be faced with resistance.*

When a requirement is placed upon an employee to make a certain change, this may imply, among other things, that a task has not been completed to the expected standard. This can be perceived as a 'negative' approach. However, when employees are able to see the benefits and understand and accept the reasoning behind why changes need to be made, they are likely to be more willing to make those changes. This means it is important for a manager to use the positive approach when encouraging staff to adopt any proposed changes.

From the very beginning, the manager must make it clear to employees that:

> *It is not about working harder, but working smarter.*

When you're sick, you will ask your medical doctor for advice on how to get better. But in the business environment, you don't have to wait till you're 'sick' to try to get better – you can focus on continuous improvement. A manager should believe that although their employees are performing well, there is always room for improvement. It's important for managers to make it clear to their employees that the quest for making improvements is not a judgment that says that something is wrong. Rather, it is about going from 'good to great', as Jim Collins wrote in his famous book of that title. In other words, it is about becoming better and better. This is why, under the MILL model, the language used to describe interventions does not refer to behavioural changes, but rather to **action improvements.**

THE FOUR AREAS OF ACTION IMPROVEMENT

Action improvement under the MILL model has four dimensions. It implies that you can do something:

1. **More:** This is about the number of times activities are performed. The expectation is that by increasing the frequency of performing certain activities, results will improve.

2. **Better:** This is about improving the quality of the activities. The expectation is that by having more of an eye for detail, results will improve.

3. **Different:** This is about a change of direction and attempting to do things in a different way. The expectation is that by doing things differently and in a more creative way, results will improve.

4. **Less/stop:** This is about re-allocating time to see where it can be saved. The expectation is that by improving efficiency and allowing more time for other activities, results will improve.

The selection of which action improvement should be explored in more detail is best determined by asking questions based on these four options. The question that is most endorsed by the team can thereafter be discussed in more detail. Below is an example for developing action improvements on telephone acquisition in a case where the impact (results vs. efforts) has been meagre so far.

1. **More:** Could the end result have been improved if we were to make more telephone calls?

2. **Better:** If we were to stick to the current levels of calls made, could we determine how the quality of calls can be improved?

3. **Different:** If we expect that doing things more or better may not work, could we consider another way of customer engagement, e.g. organising a workshop or breakfast meeting?

4. **Less/stop:** Are we able to spend our time more efficiently by using a quicker assessment of whether there is potential?

There are no right or wrong answers here. There is, however, an ongoing quest to try to identify what action improvements can be made and which approach is likely to work best.

> *Action improvement needs to be oriented towards future outcomes.*

No time should be wasted on laying blame on someone else for poor performance so far, but rather opportunities to make improvements in the future should be identified. Even those who are already performing well should be challenged to continually improve their performance, and to share successes and lessons learned with the rest of the team in terms of their application of more, better, different or less.

IMPLEMENTING ACTION IMPROVEMENT

Since most people prefer to stay within their comfort zones, action improvement faces various challenges. People may have developed beliefs about why certain behaviours are more appropriate or why new behaviours are not worth the effort. But there are some rules that can be applied in order to stretch people without causing them to become stressed. These will be explored in more detail throughout the book, but let's go through an overview of them before we move on.

1. **Make steps smaller to allow employees time to build up their confidence.** Some employees stopped learning after leaving school, whether intentionally or through circumstances. In these instances, allow for quick wins by making steps smaller in order to guarantee success and make learning and improving fun again.

2. **Clarify the expected direction, but empower employees to provide insights on how to get there themselves.** In order to get employees 'in the driving seat', they have to learn how to 'navigate' for themselves. Employees who rely on 'sat-nav management' to provide them with directions and coordinates will never learn to find their way on their own.

3. **Ensure the small steps are appreciated by recognising progress and direction.** Just as toddlers are complimented and praised when they take their first small steps, adults also need recognition when they are being stretched beyond their comfort zone. This is to encourage them to continue practising new skills.

4. **Employees should become aware of the relationship between activity and outcome in order to learn and grow.** Once employees see for

themselves the positive impact they have had on the outcome, and they get a true sense of what works well in bringing about this result, they will continue on this journey of improvement. Soon, they will no longer require as much support from their managers, nor will as much effort be required from them.

A manager who is able to coach and guide employees in taking these small steps to improve behavioural changes and focus on action improvements on a weekly basis will create successful employees who are not only motivated, but also proud.

Action improvement is for managers too.

A manager who leads by example will also show action improvement in leadership and employee engagement.

The more, better, different or less approach can be applied regardless of whether improvements are required at the employee or management level. And when management also uses the more, better, different or less approach, it reinforces the interactive learning leadership culture throughout the organisation because everyone speaks the same language and has to go through the same motions for true team-play.

For example, the process of addressing complicated issues, such as insufficient trust, during meetings can be broken down into action improvements. Trust is created as a result of certain behaviours, or because of the absence of certain behaviours. It does not make sense to spend too much time discussing the past because nobody can change it, and such discussions are only worth having if something can be learned that helps to provide ways to implement future improvements.

- What can management do *more* of to create trust (what are they not doing often enough)?

- What can management do *better* to create trust (the intention may be good but is the execution poor)?

- What can management do *differently* to create trust (what has not already been tried that is worth trying)?

- What can management do *less of* or *stop* to create trust (if performing certain activities ruins trust, should they be stopped)?

When using the more, better, different or less approach, it is anticipated that meetings will not only be more focused and specific, but as a result they will also be quicker and an improved outcome will be achieved.

ENGAGEMENT EXCELLENCE
(EMPLOYEE/EXECUTION)

Engagement
excellence

| Understand/
Needs | Update/
Expectation | Undertake/
Execution | Up to
satisfaction/
Experience |

Engagement excellence aims at embedding service excellence throughout an organisation to create a consistent customer experience. Any engagement should focus on the needs of the engagement partner, manage expectations, execute as committed and check the overall experience.

The four building blocks of engagement excellence can be practised by applying ForYou/4U as specified above. Internal clarity on expected engagement excellence can be used for external commitment. This will allow for monitoring the engagement process in order to manage customer service much better.

MANAGEMENT
MASTER MIND

CHAPTER 4

ENGAGEMENT EXCELLENCE

'The more you engage with customers,
the clearer things become and the easier it is to
determine what you should be doing.'

JOHN RUSSELL

The third blade of the MILL model is called engagement excellence. This re-fers to the quality of interaction held between people both inside and out-side an organisation. When managers and employees engage with each other within the organisation, they are referred to collectively as 'internal custom-ers'. When employees engage with customers outside an organisation, they are referred to collectively as 'external customers'. However, the term 'engage-ment partner' will be used in this book to refer to both internal and external customers, as the principles of engagement excellence are applicable for both.

Engagement excellence, in terms of taking proper care of key stakeholders, has always been important, but the importance is increasing in this age of digital disruption. Markets are nowadays more transparent, and the days when competitive advantage was based on exclusive knowledge is vanishing.

> *Engagement excellence with the external customer is often now the most important factor that differentiates an organisation from its competitors. Today, innovations are much easier and quicker to replicate and only provide a short-term competitive advantage.*

Sales and services are intertwined; therefore, it is necessary to optimise the level of service through engagement excellence in order to achieve sales excellence. Because internet and digital sales and service don't require as much personal interaction with customers, the quality of these limited engagements should be of a very high standard regardless of who is representing the organisation – whether it's an executive, a call centre agent or a service engineer. The concept of the weakest link determining the strength of the chain is also applicable here.

If front office employees show engagement excellence towards external customers, but do not receive the proper internal support needed to enable them to execute and follow up with customers, the overall result will remain poor.

Engagement excellence should be implemented throughout the entire organisation to become an LHPO.

THE FOUR STEPS OF ENGAGEMENT EXCELLENCE

Engagement excellence can be broken down into a sequence of four steps, which can be applied in engagements with both internal and external customers.

- **Step 1: Understanding needs.** This first step is to get to know more about the engagement partner's current situation, as well as what their expectations are in terms of the outcome of the engagement: what is their goal, what will change as a result and why is this important? Accurate capturing of their needs is crucial, as this information will guide the rest of the process.

- **Step 2: Managing expectations.** Once there is an accurate understanding of the engagement partner's needs, the next step is to offer an explanation of the whole process, step by step, from beginning to end. Explain what the internal and external dependencies and requirements are and what will happen next. Advise them how the follow-up will be managed, what the expected timelines are and what the end result will look like. This commitment should be captured and used as a guide during the next step – execution. It is important to keep a record of any commitments made during the managing expectations phase to ensure these are also being met.

- **Step 3: Executing in line with commitment.** After having discussions about what the engagement partner's requirements are and when agreements are made, employees will be able to manage their engagement partner's expectations by conducting proper follow-up to ensure that they, the employees, 'walk the talk' and do what they said they would do. The objective of this is to exceed expectations, especially in areas where the engagement partner's priorities lie. Any delays in timelines must be communicated to the engagement partner, and before delivery takes place quality checks must be conducted to confirm that their needs and expectations are in alignment. Generally, cost becomes less relevant for customers as long as other requirements are met in an excellent manner.

- **Step 4: Checking and improving the overall experience.** After delivering what was agreed, the engagement partner's perception of the entire interaction and its execution should be checked. There is always room for improvement, especially when the goal is to achieve engagement excellence. When the customer can immediately identify and share improvement opportunities directly with an employee, there is no need to wait for a customer survey to be completed. This type of feedback is valuable and can suggest what kind of action improvements can be implemented as 'lessons learned' in subsequent engagements.

> The four steps of engagement – Needs, Expectations, Execution and Experience – will from now on be referred to as the N(EX)3 approach for engagement excellence: N = Needs, and (EX)3 = Expectations, Execution, Experience.

The steps in the N(EX)3 approach are not strictly sequential. You may have to go backwards and forwards between Step 1 (understanding needs) and Step 2 (managing expectations), until both needs and expectations have been established and are in alignment. Managing expectations is also about making sure explanations about processes (Execution) are not only communicated clearly enough, but are acceptable and in line with the engagement partner's needs. To avoid disappointment, clarity on what to expect and the capability of the organisation during execution should also be aligned. Where expectations are unrealistic or too high, these should be managed by providing further clarification about what is realistic.

> Small mistakes made in the engagement excellence process can weaken the overall experience. Every step counts, and failure in any one of the four areas cannot always be compensated for in the other steps.

Good attention to detail is imperative, as can be seen in the following example in which a fine dining experience is spoiled.

The waiter is very attentive and enthusiastic, the food is excellent and top-quality wines are being served. Once the meal is over the guests asks for the bill, but despite several reminders the waiter fails to bring it. After waiting over thirty minutes, the evening is completely spoiled by the waiter's lack of attention to one small detail. The N(EX)3 approach recommends asking customers not only whether they enjoyed their food, but also about their overall perception of their dining experience once payment is made. This is necessary in order to provide complete and valuable feedback about where improvements can be made.

MEASURING ENGAGEMENT EXCELLENCE

Customer engagement can only be managed and improved if there are key performance indicators or benchmarks against which progress can be tracked. Customer service (quality of engagement) has traditionally been monitored by conducting checks to establish whether employees are doing such things as smiling and greeting, or by asking customers for their 'net promoter score', which reflects whether an organisation would be recommended or not. This kind of information is difficult to use for immediate improvements, however, as it is either too subjective or too vague.

> *The strength of the N(EX)3 approach for engagement excellence is that every step in the process can be measured and monitored.*

In the MILL model, engagement excellence is measurable because the N(EX)3 approach is crisp and clear. Although employees already request feedback during the experience step, it is recommended that management still conducts an additional, independent inspection on whether the N(EX)3 approach was followed, and whether any other comments and/or recommendations can be made. Below are some examples of four questions in line with the N(EX)3 approach that the engagement partner can be asked on behalf of management.

1. *Did we understand your* **needs?** *How do you rate our efforts in gaining an understanding of how we could provide you with the best service?* (This question relates to your needs, expected timelines or other expectations and whether we showed sufficient interest and a good understanding of what is most important to you.)

2. *How well did we manage your* **expectations?** *How do you rate our explanation and clarification of what you could expect from us?* (This questions whether we provided you with relevant information about what the result would look like, how long it would take to achieve and what processes would be followed, with reference also to your specific needs or what is important to you.)

3. *Was the* **execution** *as expected? How do you rate the end result? Did we execute your request effectively and did the result meet your expectations?* (This questions whether we delivered what you needed and whether the process of delivering was effective and, because you knew what to expect and when, without 'surprises'.)

4. *How was your overall* **experience?** *To help us to determine how we could improve our services, how do you rate your overall engagement with our organisation?* (This questions your perception of us and looks for suggestions about how we can improve and offer you a better service. We believe there is always room for improvement, so all suggestions or remarks are welcome.)

Besides the request for a rating, every question should have two sub-questions:

a) *Do you have any further clarification on the rating?* (What is your rating for needs, expectations, etc., based upon?)

b) *Do you have any further comments or recommendations?* (What could we still do, or should we do going forward, in terms of understanding needs, managing expectations, etc?)

The quantitative and qualitative outcome of the N(EX)3 survey should be used not only as input for the learning cycle, but also for benchmarking and performance management.

> *Employees should not only have financial indicators included in their performance assessment, but also N(EX)3 customer satisfaction scores. N(EX)3 is a more predictive indicator of future customer retention or cross-sell opportunities.*

N(EX)3 is a very powerful approach when aiming for engagement excellence. It is not only beneficial, but necessary for an organisation that wants to become an LHPO. The process is clear, so it can be monitored and applied throughout the organisation. If applied well, the N(EX)3 engagement excellence approach will become part of the organisation's DNA.

CARE & CONTROL
(MANAGER/EXECUTION)

Care & control

The aim of showing care and control is to support and encourage employees taking ownership for action, analysis (learning) and improvement. CARE is related to the person, and therefore 'softer' and more supporting; stretching is part of personal development. CONTROL is focussed on the tasks, and therefore 'harder' and more challenging; stretching is part of aiming for high performance, getting the best out of employees.

Progress
- Kicked off activity as agreed?

Impact
- Achieved deliverables to see impact?

Analysis
- Root cause, best practice or lessons learned are clear?

Feedback
- Support and stretch for further growth and grooming!

'If you don't care, I don't care.' A manager has to walk the talk to show that what is expected also will be inspected. Being on the ground as a manager and understanding what is happening makes it easier to be understood when further stretching of employees is required – and possible.

MANAGEMENT
MASTER MIND

CHAPTER 5

CARE AND CONTROL

*'Some talk to you in their free time and some
free their time to talk to you.'*

HPLYRIKZ.COM

The fourth blade of the MILL model is about **care** and **control**.

> *In order to keep the process of action learning going,
> the manager has a duty to organise appropriate follow-up and
> reinforcement. They must engage with all individual employees,
> regardless of their performance level.*

Managers may assume their most successful employees will automatically continue to achieve good results because they are naturally self-motivated. Most people, however, still feel the need to receive recognition for their good work in order to continue working in the same capacity or to the same standards. And even sales staff who are high achievers and excellent performers will, at some point, lower the bar and lose motivation if they do not receive the recognition or support they deserve from their superiors.

The manager has to continue showing care and control all the time. When managers start to 'drop the ball' and lower their level of commitment or engagement, employees may perceive it as acceptable to lower their own standards as well. The manager has a duty to inspect what they expect (see

Chapter 2) and must be seen to be consistent in all aspects of leading and engaging with the team. That said, the manager should 'walk the talk' – not just say what is important, but also act upon what they say is important. A manager whose actions don't match their words is like a parent who repeatedly requests a child to tidy up a room, but doesn't check that it's been done. If there is no follow-up or consistency in making that request, the parent's action transmits a completely different message. How likely are children to clean up their rooms if they are not being checked?

Pleasing their superior should not necessarily be a manager's first priority. Rather, a manager should make sure that they get the best out of their team by showing care and control. When staff experience very little support and attention from their managers, they may think: 'If you don't care, I don't care'. This belief can quickly spread throughout the organisation. For example, when managers of supporting departments no longer 'care' about their employees, these employees will also lose interest and become less supportive to other departments in the business. Where limited internal support is received by customer-facing departments, these departments will also lower their efforts.

> *In order to keep the process of action learning going, the manager has a duty to organise appropriate follow-up and reinforcement. They must engage with all individual employees, regardless of their performance level.*

Lack of care by a manager will always trickle down and could quickly spread throughout the whole organisation like a contagious disease.

Therefore, it is recommended that care and control is top-down and endorsed throughout the organisation. Again, the weakest link determines the strength of the chain; one badly managed, underperforming department could have an impact on the whole organisation.

THE FOUR AREAS OF CARE AND CONTROL

The four areas of care and control relate to interactions between the manager and their employees in terms of verifying progress made, identifying the impact of action commitments, requesting analysis and providing feedback.

- **Verifying progress:**

> *Progress needs to be checked by the manager within thirty-six hours of a commitment being made. If employees fail to prepare or plan within that thirty-six-hour time frame, it may look as though they have not taken their commitment seriously.*

This will make it difficult for them to achieve what they committed to in the first place. That said, where employees have not made a start or made no progress, they should not be allowed to point fingers and blame others for their mistakes. Their focus should rather be on finding alternative ways to stick to their commitment or escalate proactively (see also 'Execute or escalate' in Chapter 3).

- **Identifying impact:** When an action commitment is met, the manager will be able to identify the impact it has had by comparing the results with the effort put into its completion.

> *Staff will feel more motivated to continue performing well when their efforts are being recognised.*

They should either keep a manual track of their activities, or have access to system-generated output indicators that will help them monitor the impact of their efforts. When employees are taught and challenged how to identify for themselves the impact their efforts have had on results, they will feel more empowered and motivated to continually make improvements where they can. This will ultimately result in their own personal development.

- **Requesting analysis:** Learning is always based on a proper understanding of why something worked well and what did not work. The manager will therefore request analysis in order to help the employee understand how progress (efforts) and impact (results) correlate.

> *Employees must be clear about the root cause of a problem or the details of what worked well and what didn't before they know where improvements can be made.*

The objective of this is to continue to build on past experiences through action learning and, as such, develop a tool box full of best practices to improve performance.

- **Providing feedback:** Employees should always be given constructive feedback. This feedback should not only be based on their achievements, but also on efforts, understanding and analysis, and any other detail that was observed and appreciated by the manager. This feedback is not meant to be a top-down assessment to qualify performance, but the manager is supposed to give feedback to strengthen the employee's own development. Some options for feedback are explaining why the task was important, what good examples of success are and what the staff member did that was appreciated.

IMPLEMENTING CARE AND CONTROL

> *In the MILL model, the care part of care and control
> is the more parental or coaching kind of approach, which focuses
> on a person's efforts. The control part of care and control is more
> of an accounting or referee kind of approach, which is focused
> on the outcome or results.*

Depending on the circumstances, and also the employee's past experiences, the manager will show either more care or more control during employee engagement. For example, junior staff, high performers or those attempting something for the first time will require more care. Employees who show a lack of discipline in their approach to doing their best, or those who keep underperforming, require more control. In both instances, it is important to have access to data for numerical proof that supports the verbal interaction. Data is crucial, but in-depth understanding of data is even more important (see Chapter 28).

> *Feedback should be based on the outcome of a task as well as on
> the efforts of the individual staff member.*

In football, when the team loses, despite working very hard, they must still be commended for their good efforts. Whereas the winning team should, despite the victory, still receive constructive feedback from their coach. It is still possible that the losing team's loss was caused by a lack of teamwork from some of the players, despite some players putting in their very best efforts during the game. It is not helpful to disqualify the entire losing team as this will not encourage any non-performers to learn from those who did work hard. If good performers are not recognised for playing well, they may not feel motivated to perform as well in the match that follows.

It is important to understand, in detail, what brought about the success or failure in order to learn from these mistakes and to recognise where improvements can be made.

This final step in the MILL model is the interaction between management and employee when showing care and control, which is focused on providing new input for another learning cycle. There are two types of lessons that can be learned. One is focused on collecting best practices and involves asking what was done that worked well. The other lesson is based on what did not work well and, by understanding the root cause, gaining clarity on where improvements need to be made.

> *Most of our valuable learning experiences are gained from previous mistakes.*

This is why it is essential to be working in a constructive and supportive environment where staff will be encouraged to openly share failures in order to learn and improve.

This chapter has introduced the four blades of the MILL model: the **learning cycle, action improvement, engagement excellence** and **care and control**. We have had a broad overview of what each blade is about and why it must be incorporated if an organisation is to become an LHPO. We've also taken a brief look at the blocks that construct each blade, which will be discussed in detail in Parts 3–6. But understanding how the four blades connect and interact is also vital if the model is to be implemented effectively, and Part 2 looks at the **key tools** and **guiding principles** that ensure this will happen.

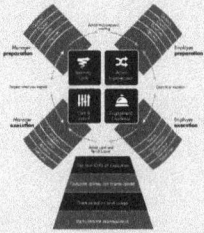

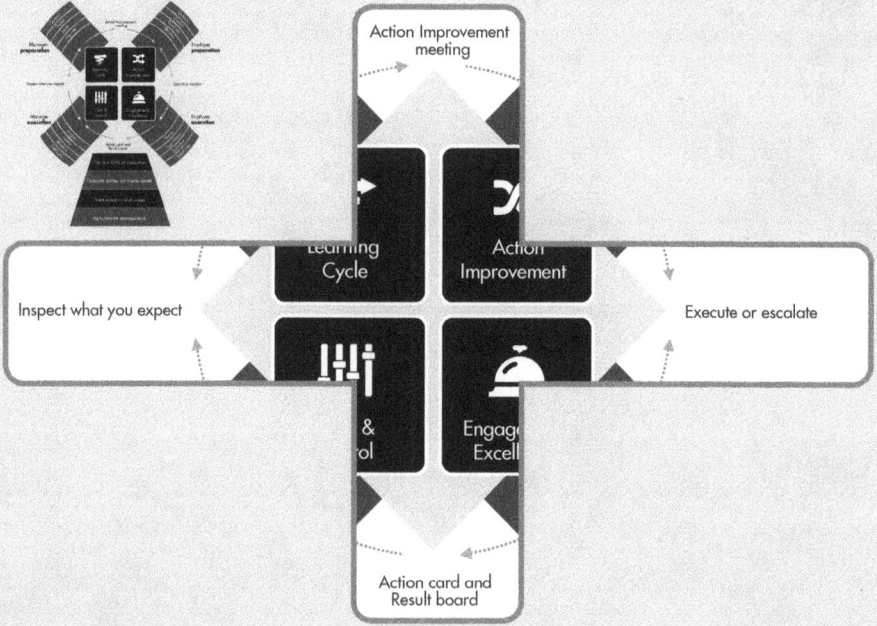

Action Improvement
meeting

Learning
Cycle

Action
Improvement

Inspect what you expect

Execute or escalate

& ol

Engag Excell

Action card and
Result board

PART 2:
CONNECTING
THE BLADES

KEY TOOLS AND GUIDING PRINCIPLES

The details of the four blades will be described in Parts 3 to 6. It is, however, important to first understand how the blades can be connected to ease the implementation of the model. This part will describe the two guiding principles and two key tools that connect the blades.

- Key tool 'Action improvement meeting' is designed to help managers and employees to come up with the best areas for improvement.

- Guiding principle 'Execute or escalate' will help employees manage their commitment well and otherwise inform their manager in a timely manner.

- Key tool 'Action card and Score board' is to track and trace action- and results-goals, as well as progress made, so that lessons can be learned and successes celebrated.

- Guiding principle 'Inspect what you expect' will help the manager to show care and control in the learning process of the employees to grow results.

Once Part 2 is implemented, it will become easier to explore further opportunities for growth and development as specified in Parts 3 to 6.

MILL MODEL KEY TOOL
ACTION IMPROVEMENT MEETING

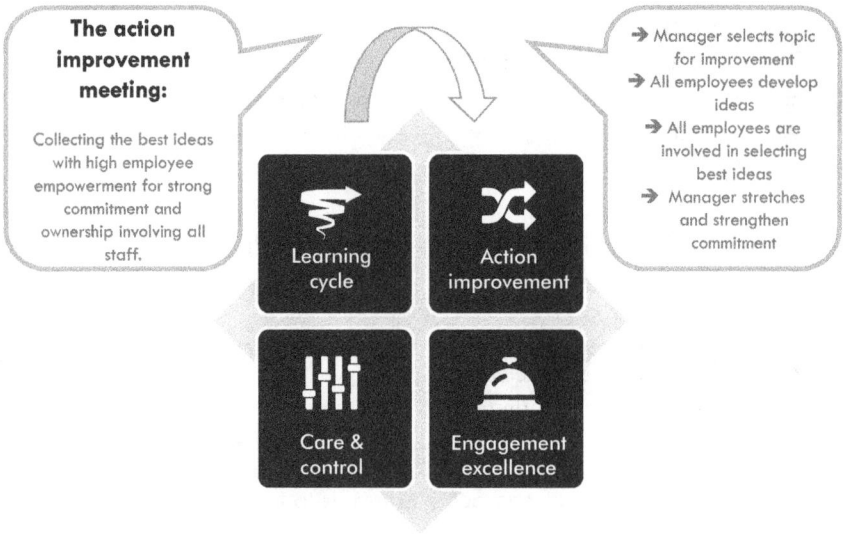

The action improvement meeting:

Collecting the best ideas with high employee empowerment for strong commitment and ownership involving all staff.

→ Manager selects topic for improvement
→ All employees develop ideas
→ All employees are involved in selecting best ideas
→ Manager stretches and strengthen commitment

Learning cycle

Action improvement

Care & control

Engagement excellence

CHAPTER 6

ACTION IMPROVEMENT MEETING

'Change is vital, improvement the logical form of change.'

JAMES CASH PENNEY

This chapter describes how the four blades of the MILL model should be linked in order to make the whole model work. First we will discuss the action improvement meeting (AIM), in which commitments are made to do things more, better, differently or less. Then we will discuss the employees' guiding principle of execute or escalate, which describes the manner in which employees will implement the commitments made in the AIM. There has to be a way for employees to track and trace their actions, and the action card and result board are designed to do just that. Finally we will look at the management guiding principle of inspect what you expect, which ensures that all of the blades of the mill are turning and will continue to turn for ongoing improvements.

Action improvements are activities with a clear aim of doing something more, better, different or less. This kind of change will not, however, come spontaneously, and top-down forcing of change by management could create resistance and lack of ownership on the part of employees. Therefore, there is a need for a balanced approach, with a weekly departmental meeting that is initiated by the manager but aims at bottom-up action improvement.

All departments in an organisation that have clear goals and objectives can make use of the AIM as a tool for agreeing on action improvements that will allow them to become more successful. It is therefore recommended that all departments make use of the AIMs, not only when they have (internal) customers, but also when management and employees of a department are willing and able to identify areas for improvement and have ambitions to go from good to great. The AIM can replace the sales or business development meetings as more ideas, more clarity for action and more commitment is created during the AIM.

Sales meetings tend to focus too much on numbers and external challenges than on determining the reasons for failures and identifying best practices that can be used for learning and improvements, agreeing on new commitments

CONDUCTING AN AIM

The weekly AIM will be conducted with the entire departmental team and should take no longer than twenty-five minutes. The focus for the week, in terms of common goals, will be discussed. Team members can have different tasks and will contribute in different ways, but there must be a common understanding of what the team is aiming for. Discussing and agreeing on the individual contributions within the team will create peer pressure and ensure employees themselves check, support and encourage each other during the week.

The steps to take for the AIM are as follows:

- **Step 1: Manager creates clarity**

    The focus for the AIM will be shared the day before the meeting is due to take place, and staff will be encouraged at that time to start developing their ideas and thoughts around the topic for the AIM. The assignment shared by the manager could for example be: what can we do more, better, differently or less this week such that we improve (measuring unit) 'X' without any further external support? 'X' could be mobile banking usage, application turnaround or anything else considered to be important and worth keeping track of.

    Once the meeting is convened, the manager starts by explaining some rules in terms of the contribution that is expected from all participants. The manager needs to clarify not only 'why' and 'what' the focus of the week is, but also what the expected outcome should look like.

> *Any idea generated by employees on how to improve action will only qualify if it can be implemented within twenty-four hours without any dependency.*

    This implies that the team does not require further support or additional resources when executing the idea, nor will it require management to make decisions. In other words, no dependency equals no excuses. Suggestions that do not meet the criteria can be appreciated, but should be deferred by the manager for discussions at a later date and in a different meeting

    For example, the outcome of the AIM can never be that the team agrees to wait until the marketing department has designed and printed a brochure.

In that case, the question for the team would be: what can the team do without a brochure, or what alternative for the brochure can be developed by the team themselves?

The rule that action improvements can and will start within twenty-four hours is not negotiable.

Even when support requests are sent to marketing, the team should not wait, but should try to see what can be done with readily available existing resources.

During the introduction, the manager will explain what the measurement unit will be in order to evaluate the results for the week. For sales people, for example, these results should preferably be to generate income. The selected topic for focus should allow results to be produced within a maximum of two weeks.

Longer term assignments should be broken down into smaller steps or pieces so that at least some progress can be expected within a two-week period.

This is comparable to building a house; the construction workers cannot commit that the house will be finished in two weeks, but they can complete the foundation in two weeks.

- **Step 2: Staff come up with ideas**
  After the manager has completed the opening message, individual staff members are given three to five minutes to individually write down, in about five to ten words, their ideas. Some employees may have more ideas than others, but they should be challenged to select or combine

the best three ideas. The time constraint of a maximum of five minutes and the obligation of writing will ensure that staff will be focused and precise, and that all employees are actively involved at this stage. While the employees are writing, the manager must walk around the room to inspect what is expected and to make sure that nobody is left out.

During the walkaround the manager will ask individual employees whether the assignment was clear enough, assess whether people are truly participating and, based on a peak over the shoulder at the ideas written so far, also get a sense of whether the individual employees have a good understanding of what is required. Some employees may have been 'hiding' during group discussions or will just pretend to be writing ideas down when, in fact, they have only written down the question.

> *By walking around, the manager ensures all employees will be challenged to contribute and makes sure that all the creativity and experience of the team will be used to get the best ideas!*

- **Step 3: Collect ideas**

  The next step of the AIM is for the manager to collate the best of all the employees' individual ideas on a flipchart in front of the group. A maximum of ten to twelve ideas should be collected within ten minutes and written clearly on the flipchart for all participants to read. This is the hardest part of the AIM in terms of time-keeping, as employees may feel that this is the time to have the kind of lengthy discussions they have had in the past.

> *It should be made very clear from the start that people are supposed to share the words they wrote on paper only; otherwise the three to five minutes spent writing does not make sense.*

If a description is still not clear, the manager can suggest different words, but there is no need to further explain or question the idea at this stage. The goal is just to collect ideas.

After an idea has been written down on the flipchart, a quick check should be done to see if it's clear for all staff. If it is, the manager should move to another employee for the next idea. The manager should alternate between staff, and in so doing encourage the more 'silent' employees to participate by encouraging them to give their input. The manager should link similar ideas from different staff members by expanding ideas that are already captured on the flipchart, instead of writing down more ideas of a similar nature. When there are roughly eight to ten ideas on the chart, the manager should start wrapping up by stating that another one or two ideas could be included if someone feels that they still have an idea that has not been mentioned, but should be included.

- **Step 4: Select Ideas**

  Based on the list of ideas generated by employees, the next step is to further empower them by allowing them to select the three ideas they like best. This selection process should not take longer than three minutes. Each member has three votes, and therefore they can vote for what they consider to be the three best ideas. The manager will number all the ideas, read every idea one more time for employees, and underline the keyword in each idea. Thereafter the manager will start the voting, line by line, by saying, 'Who is voting for number one on the list, about ...?' and stating the keyword of that idea. The number of votes for each idea will be recorded as 'strikes' in front of each idea. Once employees have given their votes for each item on the list, it will become clear which ones are considered to be the top two or three. These will be the team's agreed action improvements.

- **Step 5: Create commitment**

  In order to stay within the total time frame of twenty-five minutes, creating commitment should not take more than seven minutes. Now that the agreed action improvements are clear, more detail is required on what exactly can be expected from the employees during that same week, and therefore what will be inspected by the manager. Employees are supposed to come up with ambitious but realistic proposals on action goals that cover what will be done that same week, how much will be done, when it will be done and by whom. They should also state what result or outcome they expect to achieve by their efforts.

  It should be made clear by the manager that it is better for employees to aim high, as this stretch creates more learning, than aiming low and having an easy job with a predictable outcome.

> *Where there is a stretch, more lessons can be learned and more personal development will be achieved.*

The manager is therefore expected to challenge employees to raise the bar and really stretch themselves as part of the grooming process. More challenging targets will help to create more awareness and stronger preparation and, therefore, more success.

MANAGER'S ROLE DURING THE AIM

It's important to note that the manager takes the lead only in Steps 1 and 5. In Step 1, the manager's role is to create focus and provide an explanation of the rules, and in Step 5 to create stretching commitment. The role of the manager in Steps 2–4 has a more facilitating nature. The manager can clarify and ring-fence discussions, but should not influence the direction.

> **If the direction of discussions is too much influenced by the manager, this may disempower and alienate staff.**

If that happens, it will prevent the employees from taking ownership of both the process and their commitment to it.

> **If employees are forced to do what the manager considers the best thing from the list, they may not feel comfortable and will not own the action. They will be more successful if they are empowered to execute their first preference, even if the manager considers this the second best option, because they can act in confidence and take full ownership.**

THE BENEFITS OF THE AIM

If carried out well, the AIM will differ from a normal meeting by exhibiting the following characteristics:

- **No dominant participants, but alo no hidings:** During 'conventional' meetings, staff who are verbally stronger tend to be dominant. By making writing mandatory, a balance is created; the quieter members feel more empowered to contribute their ideas because they are not being dominated by their vocally stronger peers. Those that prefer to stay on the background are encouraged not to 'hide' behind the more vocal members and are expected to participate as much as everyone else. This ensures a much higher usage of the available team capability, as all employees are expected to think and contribute.

- **Buy-in on idea generation and empowerment in selection:** Employees are in the lead in that they are asked to come up with their own ideas rather than being directed or influenced to carry out those of their manager. Because employees are encouraged to select and utilise their own ideas, there will be more ownership of the implementation as well as a higher sense of empowerment. The manager may want to emphasise this by explaining that, 'These are your ideas and you as a team decided what you believe are the best ideas. You were asked for your commitment on actions and results. All in all, this is your plan, so you can make it work.'

- **Action-orientation and clearly defined actions and result goals:** It is made clear from the beginning that this is not a meeting for lengthy discussions or hiding behind dependencies on other departments. The goal is to achieve commitment for actions and results. Any issues requiring more time for discussions and more support will be picked up in a different meeting, thus making sure the AIM remains action-oriented.

> The outcome of the AIM is always, and for all participants, that the coming week will be different from the last week. It is guaranteed that something will be learned.

Something will be done more, better, different or less. The lesson learned will be that something either works well or can be improved.

- **Peer pressure for commitment to higher impact, team spirit and social control:** Because the AIM is conducted as a team, it creates team spirit; all members stand shoulder-to-shoulder and work on the same goals and objectives. During the week, lessons learned and best practices achieved, can be exchanged. This strengthens and benefits other members of the team by building up excitement. Working as a team creates a responsibility towards other team members, who will then start to correct and support each other in order to achieve team goals.

The AIM is a very powerful method to create commitment on actions and results while engaging and empowering staff. Conducting these meetings will require regular practice, but once well implemented, an amazing focus and ownership for actions can be achieved in just twenty-five minutes.

MILL MODEL
GUIDING PRINCIPLE FOR EMPLOYEE

Learning cycle

Action improvement

Care & control

Engagement excellence

Employee:

EXECUTE OR ESCALATE

→ Outcome of commitments has only two options: done or not done.

→ 'Not done' must never come as a surprise for the manager. Commitments that cannot be completed should be escalated as soon as possible.

→ No escalation and no execution is not acceptable; it is considered a 'breach'.

MANAGEMENT MASTER MIND

CHAPTER 7:

EXECUTE OR ESCALATE

'When you make a mistake,
there are only three things you should ever do about it:
admit it, learn from it and do not repeat it.'

PAUL BEAR BRYANT

Execute or escalate is the duty of employees to either do what has been agreed upon or, if that is not possible, inform the manager that what was agreed upon will not be done. Under the MILL model, this principle is essential to connect the commitment agreed upon in the blade of the action improvement meeting with its execution as part of the blade of engagement excellence. Commitments that should be executed or escalated are those agreed to in action improvement meetings or in coaching and feedback sessions that took place during the week.

> *The essence of the execute or escalate principle is that the manager never has to waste time reminding employees to do what they are supposed to be doing.*

The employees themselves must take ownership for their commitment, which will result in only two possible outcomes:

• **Execute:** Employees do what was agreed upon and execute the commitments made in terms of their action goals. This can also mean that time has been allocated and the proper preparation work has been done that shows they are on track. Employees are able to provide evidence that they have put in their best efforts to reach the desired outcome. In the case of setbacks, they are not simply dropping the ball and hiding behind excuses, but rather taking initiatives to overcome these challenges in order to stick to the commitment.

- **Escalate:** When it becomes clear that activities can really not be carried out as agreed, or expected timelines will not be met, the manager should be informed immediately, regardless of the reason or circumstances:

> *The manager needs to know when plans have to change or if commitments cannot be met so that expectations can be managed.*

It is not acceptable for employees to wait for the manager to check progress to find out that they have failed to stick to the commitment. That is too late. Most reasons for failing to follow through on a commitment should be accepted by the manager provided that: these failures are escalated in a timely manner; the same excuses are not used repeatedly; the same employee does not fail too often; and a new commitment is given.

It should be noted, however, that while both action and result goals are set during action improvement meetings, the execute or escalate principle is only applicable to the action goals. This is because only action goals are within the control of an employee to either execute or escalate. Result goals, in which employees are challenged to stretch and attempt new, improved ways of doing things, tend to be uncertain by nature. Therefore, there is no need to escalate result goals that have not been achieved as long as the lessons learned have been captured for sharing at a later stage.

For action goals, however, there are no options between execute or escalate. It is not acceptable for the manager to discover that employees are not executing their agreed commitments, then coming up with all kinds of excuses at the last minute when expectations and deadlines are not met. This failure is called a 'breach'. Employees should be made aware that any breach is unacceptable and may result in the manager taking action on employees who repeatedly breach their duty to execute or escalate.

MILL MODEL KEY TOOL
ACTION CARD AND RESULT BOARD

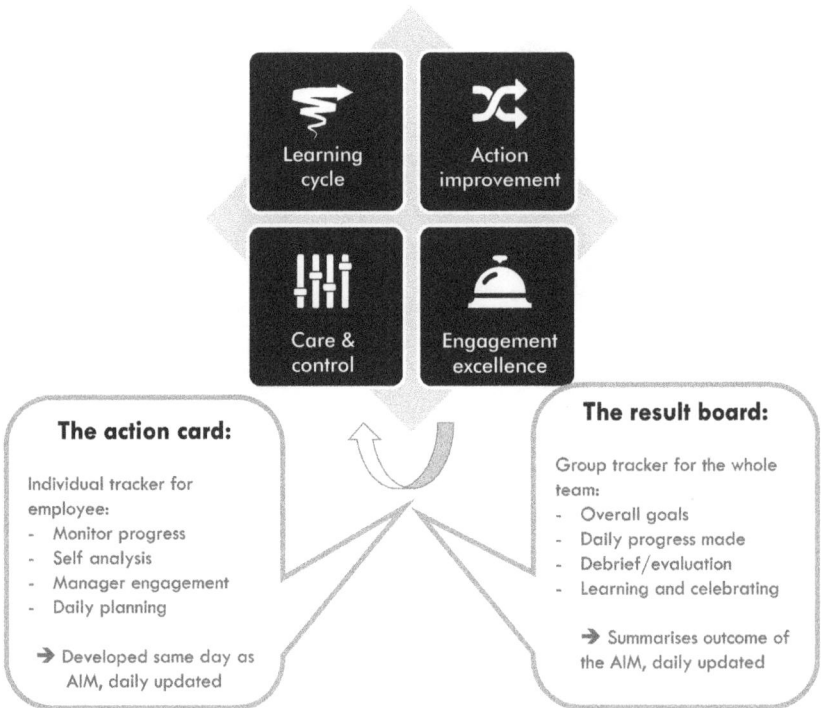

Learning cycle	Action improvement
Care & control	Engagement excellence

The action card:

Individual tracker for employee:
- Monitor progress
- Self analysis
- Manager engagement
- Daily planning

→ Developed same day as AIM, daily updated

The result board:

Group tracker for the whole team:
- Overall goals
- Daily progress made
- Debrief/evaluation
- Learning and celebrating

→ Summarises outcome of the AIM, daily updated

MANAGEMENT MASTER MIND

CHAPTER 8

ACTION CARD
AND RESULT BOARD

'That which gets measured, gets done.'

TOM PETERS

The final tools required to connect the blades in the MILL model are the **action card** and **result board** *(included in the Appendices on page 283)*, which are designed to work together. This is where employees' progress towards the commitment made in the AIM is recorded in terms of what has been agreed, what has been done, and what has been achieved. The MILL model aims at data-driven changes of behaviour; therefore, tracking and tracing really is key in making the model work.

> *Anything considered important enough to discuss should be important enough to track, and therefore should be captured on the action card or result board.*

Individual employees use an action card as their personal commitment-to-do list and to self-monitor their progress. The action card should be easily accessible to the manager to faciltate meaningful, evidence-based engagement beween manager and employee any time the manager drops by.

The result board will be updated at the end of every day by the employees themselves. The result board will be used to record the overall results of all employees for the purpose of a team review (debrief) and team learning, under the guidance of the manager, at the end of the week.

THE USEFULNESS OF TRACKING AND TRACING

When executed well, tracking and tracing can be beneficial to both managers and employees. The following examples clarify why tracking and tracing is important and how the action card and result board will add value.

- **Focus on what needs to be done**

When individuals are required to physically record their commitment on an action card, they feel encouraged to stay focused and will experience more job satisfaction as they tick a box each time their commitments are met.

This is similar to the way people organise their time in a hectic environment by using a to-do list and striking out completed activities. Having the action card on the employee's desk all the time will act as a reminder of what still needs to be done, or what the first assignment should be to start with the very next day.

- **Peer pressure**
Tracing progress in a transparent manner – on a public result board that is clearly visible to everyone – will provide an overview of all individual commitments made as well as the performance so far of each team member. This creates peer pressure among team members because they will be able to see who is in the lead and who is lagging. It is important not to judge the result, as the root causes of either over- or under-performance still need to be analysed. There should be no blame game, but an

opportunity to learn from experience. The intention is to stimulate both leading and lagging employees to perform better by understanding what worked well and what did not work. The advantage of the transparency of a result board is that lagging employees will become aware of what can be achieved when they see the results of their successful colleagues.

- **Personal development**
  Having their own individual action card should motivate and encourage employees to take ownership of their development and, in doing so, improve their performance. When employees keep track of the impact of their efforts and are therefore able to analyse the drivers of their success, they will feel pride in their work and also discover where there may still be room for improvement.

> *By comparing their individual performance with their better performing peers, employees can learn from the best to become better.*

Whether they do so with or without the manager, employees who track their results and do their own analysis will learn to understand what works well and where and how they can improve themselves even further as part of their personal development.

USING THE ACTION CARD

All employees should individually keep track of their progress on their own action card. They should capture all their commitments made during action improvement meetings and also break down the weekly target into daily targets. At the end of every day, the action card should be updated by reviewing results and lessons learned as outcomes of the actions taken. This information should be used to prepare or adjust the action planning for the following day.

Under the MILL model, both results and lessons learned are considered to be successes and therefore both are worth capturing.

Lessons learned are recommendations for improvements based on experiences of what does not work, and understanding why it did not work. Describing the situation (S), the behaviour (B) and the outcome (O) could be used for adjusted action improvements (L for learning) for the next day or next time. This is known as the SBOL framework. An example could be:

- Situation: Customer was complaining.

- Behaviour: I assured customer that I would do something extra for them, so I brought them two coffees instead of the one they asked for.

- Outcome: Customer was confused, and I had to explain that I brought the extra coffee because, from now on, I would do something extra to show our goodwill.

- Lesson learned: Humour can help break the ice, but not if the customer is too tense to appreciate the joke. When this happens, they might feel like you aren't taking them seriously.

The action card should accommodate capturing these lessons learned for personal development, engagement with the manager, and sharing with the team during the debrief at the end of the week.

USING THE RESULT BOARD

The results of the daily activity of individual employees should also be captured on the result board. This board is designed and positioned such that the team that attended the AIM can see where contributions and progress have been made. The result board provides a very quick indication of whether the execution of the commitments made, produced the expected results. The result board reflects contributions made by all employees; therefore it should also be updated by administrative and other support staff to ensure that it shows the whole department's progress in terms of teamwork.

The result board will enable employees to compare their performance with that of their colleagues on a daily basis. This helps them to determine where improvements can be made and what can be learned from their more experienced colleagues.

> *The result board can be used as a guide for staff to know who of their colleagues to approach in order to learn best practices.*

High achievers will also be recognised, as the board will make their results clearly visible to all peers. This will ensure they continue to perform at their best as they try to hold on to that leading position.

THE WEEKLY DEBRIEF

At the end of the week, the manager conducts a fifteen-minute AIM debrief with the whole team standing in front of the result board. The manager will start by summarising the action goals that have been achieved, the overall results and some highlights of the week. The individual who performed best, as well as the runner-up, should be announced. The manager can use the announcing of a runner-up to also recognise less experienced or more reserved employees. The purpose of announcing the runner-up is to make it clear that outstanding efforts, an excellent attitude or strong support is also appreciated even if the outcome is not of the highest standard (yet).

The AIM debrief is not only used for recognition and appreciation, but also for the exchange of lessons learned and best practices. Employees are therefore expected to bring their individual action cards and share their most valuable insights in terms of what works well or what does not work. This clarification should be brief to allow all employees to share, and should be done under the SBOL framework.

> *It is the role of the manager to ensure that any lessons learned and any positive results achieved are recognised. Celebrating successes helps to build a stronger team.*

The next step is to reinforce learnings by encouraging individuals in the team to apply best practices learned. The top three to five best practices that were shared during the end-of-week debrief will be captured as new commitments for all team members. To close the debriefing, the manager should announce the theme for the next action improvement meeting, and finally offer a word of thanks for the support and efforts of the whole team.

Flow chart learning process

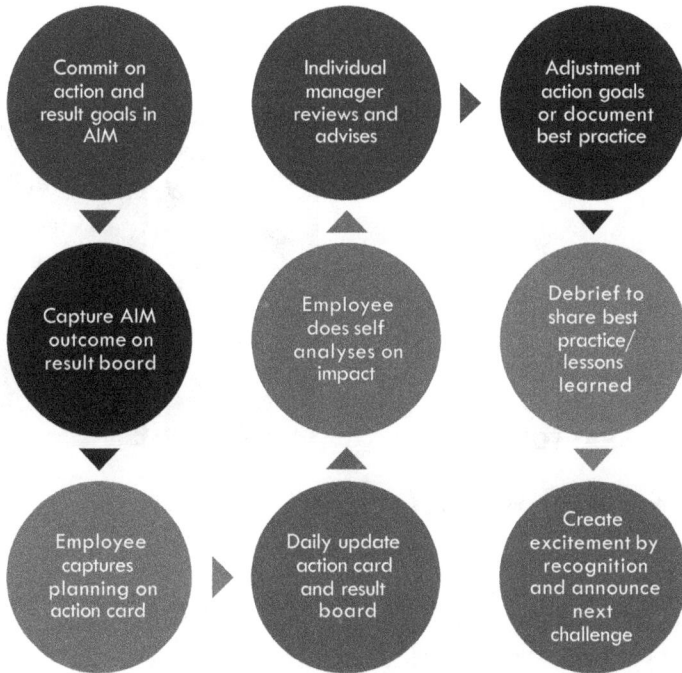

MILL MODEL
GUIDING PRINCIPLE FOR MANAGER

Learning cycle	Action improvement
Care & control	Engagement excellence

Manager:

INSPECT WHAT YOU EXPECT

→ It is the duty of the manager to clearly show what is considered to be important.

→ Improved results can only come from improved actions.

→ Only looking at results will not suffice and showing care and control for actions is essential.

CHAPTER 9

INSPECT WHAT YOU EXPECT

'People don't do what you expect, but what you inspect.'

LOU GERSTNER

For managers, **inspect what you expect** is like the 'walk the talk' of priority setting. While employees have the duty to execute or escalate, the same kind of duty is applicable for a manager to inspect what is expected. Stating the importance of an activity or goal should go hand-in-hand with managerial behaviours that show that the manager is serious about the follow-up of any commitments made. Inspect what you expect requires showing an interest both in activities that should lead to results and the outcome of efforts made.

There are short-term and long-term benefits, for both the organisation and the employee, that makes it essential for the manager to inspect what is expected.

- **Quality control**
  The quality or standard of the work and output from staff should be such that the manager never has to defend him or herself towards superiors because what is being delivered by their employees is below their own standard. Only when the manager does quality inspection by inspecting what is expected can he or she be sure that the quality meets the requirements. A manager can delegate tasks but can never delegate

responsibilities. If tasks are not executed well, the manager still has a duty to intervene in a timely manner in order to make improvements to the quality.

> *Managers who are surprised when subordinates deliver a disappointing quality of work are clearly not spending enough time inspecting what was expected.*

In football, a coach who cannot make the team perform will be fired, as a coach is expected to get the best out of players.

- **Showing you care**

The second reason why it is important to inspect what you expect is that it shows employees that you care about them. Employees tend to act on what they assume managers feel to be important based on how, where or with whom those managers spend their time. For example, if managers spend more time with senior management than with their own team, employees may begin to assume that the manager's priorities do in fact lie elsewhere, despite hearing managers say that employees are their biggest assets.

> *Employees' behaviour is driven by the notion that, 'If you don't care, I don't care'.*

When managers do not sincerely care about the performance and wellbeing of their employees, how can they expect their employees to be concerned about either the organisation's wellbeing or its performance?

- **Decision making**

  Managers in most organisations are also involved in broader decision making as they are part of management teams. Being part of such a decision-making unit requires having an in-depth understanding on what is happening on the ground and what the practical implications could be of the decisions to be made. If the manager is inspecting what is expected, then these engagements with employees will ensure this thorough understanding. Managers who are able to give immediate feedback on new proposals being discussed in management teams can show their peers and superiors that they are in control and know what they are doing.

- **Grooming**

  Grooming of employees is most effective if done by giving operational feedback about how tasks have been done or how they should be properly executed. Quick follow-up and faster feedback on (newly) executed tasks is powerful; it creates a shorter turnaround time in the learning cycles and therefore faster learning. Inspecting what you expect through personal observations allows the manager to see how much effort the employee put in to a certain task in order to achieve a particular result or outcome.

> *Teaming up with the employee to see where improvements can be made and showing support in their personal development is highly motivating.*

Whatever you pay attention to will grow; if you want your employees to grow, then pay attention and inspect what you expect.

HOW TO INSPECT WHAT YOU EXPECT

As a football coach, you not only have to watch the scoreboard to see how well the team is playing, you also have to watch the game.

Sometimes players do very well but still lose, and sometimes it is the other way around. The coach expects both effort and results, and must inspect both in order to clarify what needs to be improved. It's the same for a manager – if they believe that a training session is 'very important', then they should stay in the room during the training. If a meeting is 'really necessary', then the manager should not walk in and out all the time. If a manager qualifies a written sales plan as 'the foundation of success', then the manager has to read the plan thoroughly and give proper feedback. Inspect what you expect is showing interest and care in line with the communicated priorities.

Daily engagement by the manager is not only done to show care – the intervention should also be used for grooming and development. Providing support to employees throughout their learning process can be done in three steps:

1. Show an interest in the impact their contributions have made so far.

2. Assist them by reviewing and analysing with them the things that worked well.

3. Reach an agreement on where there is still room for improvement.

Where management fails to inspect what is expected, the perception may be created that they are not committed and will, therefore, not be taken seriously by staff. Any manager who wants to be taken seriously must make the effort to engage with their employees. A manager who merely 'assumes' employees are doing what they should be doing is not contributing towards the building up of an LHPO and needs to adopt an inspect what you expect approach.

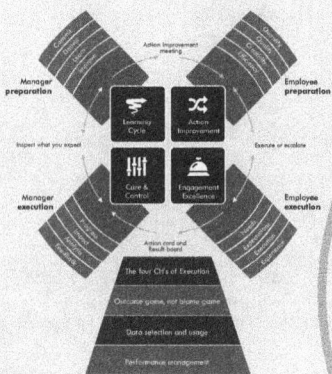

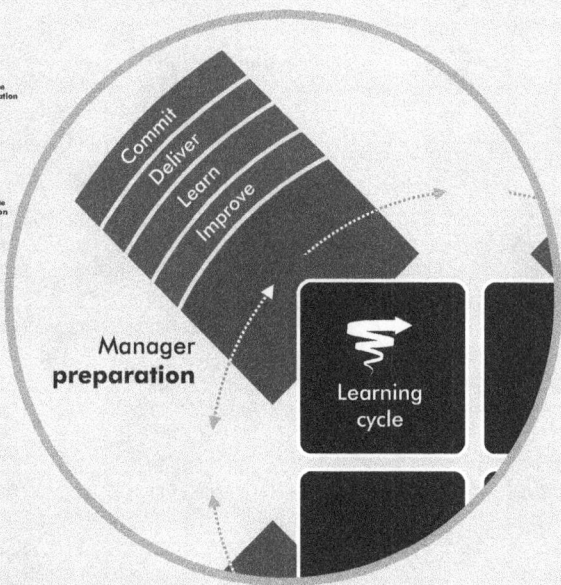

PART 3:
THE LEARNING CYCLE

Part 1 and 2 of this book gave you an overview of the blades of the MILL model and the role-guiding principles and key tools that connect the blades to keep the model working. Now we will go into more detail and look at all the building blocks that make up each blade of the model. The manager has to master these concepts, as stretching in commitment and self-reflection for improvement will not happen if the manager is not facilitating the journey for growth and development.

The first blade of the MILL model is the **learning cycle**, and is constructed of four building blocks:

1. Commit to make crisp and clear what the aim is.

2. Deliver to have clear focus that some outcome is expected.

3. Learn from both successes and failures.

4. Improve to get some benefits out of the learnings.

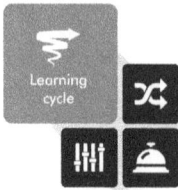

COMMIT

Strong, stretching commitment on both actions and results is the fuel for learning.

Commitment goes beyond goal setting; it also implies that accountability and responsibility has been confirmed by the employee. Being specific about action commitment and result commitment allows monitoring and improvement.

Proper commitment always has four dimensions:

How much	→ Specify how many actions and how many results
Of what	→ Describe what the action and deliverable will look like
By when	→ Plan timing of activity and estimate time of delivery
And who	→ Identify required stakeholders for success

MANAGEMENT MASTER MIND

CHAPTER 10:

COMMIT

'You must do the thing you think you cannot do.'

ELEANOR ROOSEVELT

The first building block of the learning cycle that we will look at is commitment. Commitment is strongly related to creating clarity. It has already been said that:

> **If you do not know what you are looking for, you will not find it.**

This may sound obvious and simple, but 'obvious' and 'simple' are not always the same as 'easy'. It is often assumed that there is sufficient clarity about what needs to be achieved and what the expected outcome of a commitment should be, only to find out when it is too late that it was not clear at all.

A good example of vague commitment is where an issue is discussed during a meeting and an agreement is made for someone to 'look into it'. This having to 'look into it' can mean anything and will always result in random and incomplete results. For example, when an organisation needs to 'look into' a market opportunity, it is likely that the various departments have their own expectations: the finance department expects a financial report; the marketing department expects a campaign proposal; and the risk department expects a risk assessment. When the meeting reconvenes, the sales department

– not being aware of all these expectations – has only looked at what their competitors are doing. It becomes highly likely in such situations that decision making will have to be postponed until the next meeting, as there was no clarity on what commitment was expected from the start.

> **Weak commitments will lead to inefficient meetings and poor accountability.**

The learning cycle begins the moment a proper commitment is made. This chapter provides clarity in terms of what the requirements of such commitments are in relation to the MILL model. Creating a commitment may seem similar to goal-setting, but commitment is stronger because it includes the attitude involved – commitment is also about the drive and intention to achieve. Having a plan is not, therefore, the same as having a commitment – it is just a starting point. It is necessary to take ownership of actions and results to turn a plan into commitment.

CREATING COMMITMENT

Commitment is created when the person who has taken responsibility for an assignment has a clear understanding of all relevant details required to execute the job, and confirms that it can and will be done. The more specific and detailed the instructions relating to an assignment are, the more likely it is that the employee will understand and grasp exactly what needs to be achieved. More time should be allocated during meetings so that all the relevant details are discussed. It is more productive to have a meeting with less discussion, but where proper time is spent on the details of what is expected from the commitment, than to have a meeting where too much discussion takes place and the objectives are still vague and unclear.

Commitment requires the individual to take ownership of all the details of the end result. Where there is neither interest shown nor a willingness to take ownership, any commitments made simply become 'lip service'. Even if you know what you are looking for, you will not find it unless you are serious about trying to.

> *Commitment is, therefore, focusing on both the intended actions and the expected results – you have to both know what to do and what to look for.*

The following sequence can be used to create this type of strong commitment:

- The manager makes it clear *what* should be achieved by specifying details of the expected end result.

- Employees should then be challenged and empowered to produce their own thinking and to come up with their own proposals on *how* to achieve the expected end result.

The employee should show a good understanding of what needs to be done and how much effort and time is needed to achieve the expected result. The manager can still offer support, but it should be clear that the employee has the lead once commitment has been created. If the manager determines the 'how' for staff, that is considered to be micro-managing and should be avoided in the MILL model. Consider the following example:

A manager asks an employee to deliver a parcel to the airport (here, the 'what' of the assignment is clear). It is better in such situations for the manager to allow the employee to take the route they already know, even if the manager is aware of a faster and shorter route. Allowing the employee to follow their own familiar route will ensure they don't get lost, whereas forcing the employee to take the shorter route, familiar only to the manager, could make the employee feel less confident and result in their getting lost anyway. Should this happen, the employee will feel the need to ask the manager for guidance and directions. Who is in the 'driving seat' in a situation where the manager has to step in again and again? Drivers nowadays have Google maps and car navigation systems to rely on, but as a result they tend to lose the skill of finding destinations on their own. There is a saying, 'If you don't use it, you lose it,' but it can also be said that, 'If you do not practise, you will not learn.' While the manager can provide guidance on the expected result – that is, successfully delivering the parcel – the employee has to specify the route to get there. This helps to create empowerment and ownership, and is also part of the employee's learning and personal development.

COMMITMENT TO RESULTS

During action improvement meetings, when using the MILL model, the focus should be on both actions and results, as both need to be analysed and understood to be able to measure impact. The first step is to describe in detail what the end result committed to should look like. Once this has been established, any supporting action can be validated in terms of the likelihood that it will contribute to the expected results.

The following four questions should be addressed to create a clear commitment for results:

How much? What is the quantity of the deliverable? That is, how many appointments should be made, how many units should be produced, how many controls should be conducted? This should be a number that can be measured and verified, either from the system or through manual tracking.

Of what? What is the quality and/or added value of the outcome? The result should generate some benefits and when these are understood, there will be motivation to take action. It's important to be specific. For example, instead of only asking for 'a recommendation', ask employees to 'deliver a two-page document with three options, including financials, criteria applied and a recommendation'. All participants should have the same 'picture' in their mind, based on the detailed description.

By when? Commitments should have a defined time frame for completion. Under the MILL model this should be one week where possible, to keep the momentum going for the weekly engagement. Bigger assignments that take months to be completed can be broken down into smaller steps, with partial delivery, in order to still have clear commitment on what can be expected within one week.

And who? It should be made clear who is being targeted or who is involved in achieving success. The more specific the commitment can be, in terms of the names or profiles of who will be engaged with whom, the easier it becomes to track progress. For example, 'All customers who have been loyal to us over the last five years', or, 'The numbers twenty-one to thirty on the prospect list.'

COMMITMENT TO ACTION

The following four questions, which relate to action commitment, can be derived from results commitment. Employees tend to mix up action and result goals, but when the expected results are crisp and clear it becomes much easier to see what needs to be done to achieve them. The questions that should be asked to determine the required actions are the same questions discussed above for results, but with a different focus. In this case, the answers to the questions should be about the actions that will be performed in order to achieve the expected results:

How much?   This is about what effort is required and how much time and resources need to be allocated to action the commitment. For example, this could be a daily commitment to call a certain number of prospects. If the result commitment for the week is to set up five prospect meetings for the following week, then the action commitment could be to call ten prospects. The assumption here is that half of the prospects called may not be interested in a meeting or do not have time for one.

Of what?   This is about breaking down activities in such a way that it clarifies what needs to be prepared and executed, and what follow-up should be done. In the case of calling prospects, this could be about doing some desk research, drafting a checklist, writing a script and developing a template to capture responses for follow-up.

By when?   Initial planning is required, and it is recommended that this begins within thirty-six hours of a commitment being made.

Otherwise it is unlikely that the expected results willbe achieved in time. Time needs to be allocated for the action improvement that was agreed. For example, it can be assumed that, at around noon, prospects may be less busy and not yet out for lunch (expect for Fridays). Therefore, at least four prospects will be called around this time. By calling at this time towards the beginning of the week, there will be time for corrective measure before the end of the week if the response is poor.

And who?   Addressing dependencies on support is recommended, but only if it is also explained how these dependencies are expected to be managed. In the example above, a detailed list of prospects and names of executives can be prepared, and employees who are to call the prospects should inform their colleagues that they should not be disturbed between 12.00 and 12.30 every day.

In summary, during action improvement meetings employees agree what will be done more, better, different or less. However, the detail of the action commitment should not be discussed in the meeting, and action commitments could also differ slightly among employees. During the AIM, it is recommended to at least agree upon the results commitment for each employee.

After the meeting, employees may need some time to develop a more detailed commitment on what actions are required to achieve the results committed to using the questions 'How much, Of what, By when, And who?'. These action commitments will thereafter be checked by the manager during the first individual follow-up meeting, using the action card.

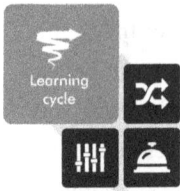

DELIVER

Delivering is the creation, by the employee, of any tangible outcome by the execution of a commitment.

It is important that employees really try their best in terms of proper preparation, engagement and follow-up. Deliverables should be such that outcome can be used for learning and improvement.

Delivering is the outcome of a process

Planning/preparation ➔ Making sure to be as ready as possible

Engagements ➔ Executing the core activity with best effort

Follow-up/tracking ➔ Making it clear what is scheduled next

Analysis/results ➔ Monitoring outcome to understand impact

CHAPTER 11:

DELIVER

'Every accomplishment starts with the decision to try.'

JOHN F KENNEDY

The previous chapter described the first step of the learning cycle and how to create commitment for both actions and results. The second step of the cycle is for the employees to act on this commitment – in other words, this is where the targeted execution takes place. **Delivering** is not about executing tasks at random and doing things for the sake of doing things, but rather is a focused process with a clear goal in mind.

The word **deliver** is used intentionally as a way to highlight the fact that a tangible outcome of some kind is expected. Both (tangible) results and (tangible) lessons learned qualify as a **deliverable**, as the organisation should always be able to benefit from deliverables, either immediately or in the future. It is made clear by the manager from the outset that something tangible needs to be delivered during the week in order to demonstrate effort, and also to have an input for comparison between efforts and impact to enable learning and further improvement

> *Delivering in the learning cycle is about doing something more, better, different or less – in other words, something beyond the 'normal'.*

Generally speaking, any new activity requires more effort, which makes these kinds of behavioural changes difficult. Therefore, the manager should show care and control by making themselves available to support and encourage employees, where needed, as they stretch while aiming for some deliverable. Breaking the delivery assignment down into smaller steps helps the manager to determine more easily and in a more effective way what can be expected and, therefore, what needs to be done in terms of inspecting what is expected.

If the manager is not closely involved during the deliver phase, it may be difficult to determine whether a failure was due to expectations being set too high, or simply down to the sub-standard execution of tasks. This goes back to the example of the football coach, who has to watch the game to see how individual players performed to be able to do a proper assessment of areas for improvement.

> *The manager has to show care by interacting closely with employees during the week in order to understand what the root causes of the successes or failures were.*

THE FOUR STEPS OF DELIVERING

If a task has been committed well but poorly executed, it's still unlikely to be successful. The principle that 'the chain is only as strong as the weakest link' is also relevant when applied to the execution of a task. Below is an overview of the four steps of delivering.

1. **Creating bite-size steps**

   The first step after an action improvement meeting is to understand where to start in order to create some traction. Generally, employees tend to procrastinate when an assignment appears to be a challenge, as if it is a mountain that needs to be climbed. The process of undertaking a task will become more achievable and faster once it is broken down into smaller steps. Quick successes also help employees feel that the new approach is working; this will create momentum for them to take on more challenging tasks. These quick wins can only be achieved if larger commitments are broken down into smaller, partial deliverables.

2. **Planning/preparation**

   Staff may find it difficult to allocate time to perform tasks that are assigned to them on top of their ongoing activities. However, by referring to their own commitment made during the action improvement meeting and allowing them to make their own planning, they should be able to prepare for delivery. The employee has to make sure that sufficient time is allocated and the right support is organised to ensure action commitments will be met and some deliverables will be achieved. Preparation is also about making sure that the required knowledge and tools are in place in terms of what to ask, what to say and what to do during the engagement and execution of tasks.

3. **Engagement/execution**

   This is the activity itself as described and agreed to in the action improvement meeting. It is important for employees to be able to go through some self-reflection right after the engagement/activity in order to develop awareness of what has actually happened during the engagement/

activity. The employee should reflect on what went well and what did not go well, and therefore what can be improved in the next engagement/action. The quality of engagement can be assessed by asking self-reflection questions on whether there was a good understanding of the needs of the engagement partner, whether their expectations of what can or will be done were managed properly, and whether follow-up was done as agreed. Another powerful way to find out how it went is simply asking for input from the engagement partner to see whether their expectations have been met and whether they had a good overall experience.

4. **Follow-up/tracking**

The opportunity for a more successful outcome will be far greater if relevant engagements are followed up soon after engagements. Therefore, any issues arising out of these conversations should also be noted and followed up immediately. It doesn't take a lot of effort to follow up after conversations take place, and the results are well worth it in terms of retaining customers. As most organisations fail to do such quick follow-up, this is a quick win that shows the organisation is serious and makes a real difference by exceeding expectations. The manager should encourage employees to use a tracking and tracing system, ensuring that opportunities or new commitments will be executed within the agreed time frame.

In summary, the manager can find out where the employee can improve by asking questions or making suggestions based on these four steps of delivering. Where the preparation or follow-up of a task is poor, the expected result is unlikely to be achieved. It could be useful to break any substantial tasks down into small sections to be able to act faster and with more focus on failure or poor performance. The manager should check with the employee whether there is some understanding of what went well and what did not go well. There is always room for improvement, so even top performers will be challenged to see where improvements can be made in each of the four steps of the delivery process.

AVOIDING EXCUSES

The focus of Step 2 in the learning cycle is to come up with deliverables, and it's important that employees avoid making excuses or blaming others for non-performance when action or results commitments are not met. It is too easy to get into the habit of blaming others when things don't go as expected or are being presented as beyond one's control. These kind of explanations, where the employee makes it look like nothing can be done and a lot of talking is done to explain why something did not happen, is called storytelling and should not be tolerated.

> *The spirit should be that every non-achievement or failure provides a lesson to be learned that can be used for future development.*

To support their employees, the manager should avoid blaming employees for the past, but rather make them accountable for the future.

When the focus is on things that haven't happened or on what hasn't been achieved, changes cannot be made because the employee has chosen to live in the past. Employees should be encouraged to replace negative conversations about what went wrong with positive ones about what has been learned and where improvements can be made.

> *We cannot change the past, but what we have experienced so far, can become beneficial to us if we can learn from it and we take action to improve.*

Our experiences should motivate employees to take ownership for what work still needs to be done without being dependent on anyone else. People who make excuses generally avoid accepting responsibility, and this means that their ability to learn or make improvements is hindered. A manager should intervene when employees make excuses and change excuses into action improvements.

This second step in the learning cycle – delivery – provides opportunities to acknowledge positive achievements and also identify areas that require further learning and development. As long as employees are able to identify what they have learned by following the process, and continue to make commitments to improve, they are 'off the hook' as results will eventually follow when ownership is shown for ongoing improvement.

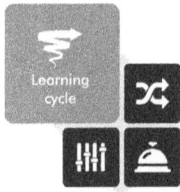

LEARN

There is always something that can be learned. Probably the best lessons come from the biggest failure, but even small challenges can be used to learn and become better.

Mistakes and challenges are like mirrors for personal growth. Look at them to understand where they come from and address them!

There are four possible lessons that can be learned when comparing actions and results:

→ You realise that **WHAT** was done was not enough

→ You learned that **HOW** it was done was not optimal

→ You discovered **WHERE** to change because the approach did not work

→ You clarified **WHICH** activity did not add value or was too cumbersome

CHAPTER 12:

LEARN

*'Success is not delivering a feature,
it is learning how to solve the customers' problem.'*

ERIC RIES

After **commit** and **deliver**, the next step in the learning cycle is to **learn**. The MILL model, which is based on learning by doing (a.k.a. action learning), implies that learning from experience is the most powerful way of learning because multiple senses can experience the impact of the effort.

> *Learning starts by comparing the achievements
> (deliver) to the planning (commit).*

This will be done for both the actions and results that were committed to during and immediately after the action improvement meeting. The commitments made were very specific in terms of how much, of what, by when and who. Proper tracking of what worked well and what did not work was done during the delivery phase, which means that all components are set up for evaluation and learning.

> *The intention of the learn phase is to help identify not only
> root-causes for challenges that may arise, but also understand why
> certain actions created good results.*

Before explaining the differences between symptoms and root causes and the relevance for proper learning, however, it should be made clear why the focus should be on both what is going well and what is not.

There is a tendency for management to focus more on an employee's shortfalls than their successes. For example, if the employee's score is 'green', it means the employee has successfully achieved their objectives. If the score is 'red', the employee has not achieved a successful outcome and needs to provide an explanation why. A report that shows both 'smileys' and 'sad faces' will only be discussed to find out where people have failed for the areas where there are 'sad faces'. Because the focus is on the negatives, this approach may cause resistance. Employees may tend to point fingers and blame someone else for any failures and, therefore, resist taking ownership of doing a better job the next time.

But lessons can be learned from both successes and failures; therefore, a more balanced approach is recommended. Under the MILL model, it is important to understand how success has been achieved and how it can be replicated.

> *Activities that resulted in successes can be broken down into smaller steps so the organisation can build a common understanding of its best practices.*

The purpose of identifying best practices is to explore opportunities to apply the same experiences elsewhere. Best practices can be:

- Repeated by the person who developed them.

- Imitated when used by different employees.

- Copied in terms of using the same best practice approach for a different, more challenging setting.

- Perhaps even improved on in the quest for moving from good to great.

Best practices are manuals for success, so it is strongly recommended not only to share best practices but also translate them into new action commitments the very moment they are being shared.

SYMPTOMS VERSUS ROOT CAUSE

These two terms are common terminology in the medical world. A general practitioner examines a patient by looking for symptoms. The root cause of a disease can often be hard to detect because it lies inside the body and is not visible from the outside. Some symptoms may, however, be displayed externally and point to where the real problem, or root cause, may be. The GP observes and carries out practical experiments to help identify symptoms of the problem – gently hitting the patient's knee; shining a light into their eyes; looking into their throat; listening to their lungs.

The GP has learned through study and experience which symptoms point to certain root causes of a disease, and also which ones could exclude the possibility of a certain disease being present.

When comparing the commitments made in terms of actions and results with the achievements or outcome, it may also not be immediately clear what the root causes or reasons for under-achievement or success are. More observations can be made when breaking action and result assignments down into smaller steps. Digging deeper into understanding what really happened may also bring the root causes of over- or under-performance to the surface. Digging deeper can be done by asking the relevant 'why' questions. For example:

Employee: 'There was not enough time.'

Manager: 'Why did you not have enough time?'

Employee: 'Because I still had some details to check as the file was not complete.'

Manager: 'Why was the file incomplete?'

Employee: 'Because they did not put all the history in the file.'

Manager: 'Why did they not put all the history in the file?'

Employee: 'Because I was not clear what I was looking for.'

Etc, etc, etc.

Once these questions have been answered, it may be seen that poor preparation and/or poor instructions were the root causes of the problem. Any attempts to point fingers or place blame for failure on someone else should be avoided or will at least require more questioning by the manager on what still *could*, and therefore *will* be done by the employee.

If we don't understand the reasons for failure or success, we will not be able to learn and grow, nor will we be able to explore drivers of successes in order to make further improvements.

FOUR CATEGORIES FOR LESSONS LEARNED

The goal of this step is to understand what caused a gap between commit and deliver.

That is, what was done too much, or what wasn't done enough.

The learn phase is intended to generate input for the improve phase; therefore, self-reflection is key.

Time should not be wasted on having discussions about what others can or can't do, or should or shouldn't do. How other people behave should be considered circumstantial, so we need to either live with it or work around it. The only person that you can really change is yourself. It is right to provide suggestions for how other people in the room should change, but discussing these when people involved are absent is a waste of time and counter-productive. People love to have long discussions and agree on what other people should do, but these discussions are completely useless and should be avoided.

> *Lessons can be learned and answers provided by analysing*
> *symptoms and understanding the root causes for failures.*

To do this, simply ask one or more of the following categories of questions:

- **What questions**
  These apply when what was achieved is not sufficient. The reason could have been insufficient time for completing the task, or not enough interactions taking place with the customer. This could have been down to sub-standard planning, insufficient time being allocated to a task or

too much attention focused on activities that could have been rescheduled. 'What was the real problem?'

- **How questions**

  These should be asked when an employee learns that the way they completed a task was not to the best of their ability but, had it been performed in a different way, the results may have been different or even better. Perhaps more time could have been spent on either the preparation of the task, or in gaining a better understanding of the background and expectations of the customer concerned. If more research had been conducted into what was expected, it may certainly have resulted in the employee being better prepared, and the pitch or presentation given to the customer greatly improved. 'How could you improve?'

- **Where questions**

  If a specific approach fails to work, the employee may learn to detect where adjustments could have been made. Perhaps the wrong people were working on the task, or there was a failure even to understand the level of detail required for the proposal. It could also have been due to an incomplete proposal that failed to include relevant competitor analysis and proper alternatives, resulting in an inability to make a decision. 'Where in the process will improvements have the highest impact?'

- **Which questions**

  By asking these it becomes clear which activities did not add value or were too cumbersome. It is said that 'less is more', and in order to make improvements it is helpful to understand where time could be spent in a more efficient and effective way. Each engagement for sales or support has a number of steps, but they are not equally important. For this reason, it is important to constantly streamline processes as part of the learning process. 'Which activity did not add that much value?'

The learn phase requires a certain amount of constructive self-examination, which can only be achieved by focusing on understanding the root causes of a certain outcome. Employees should not be blamed for past mistakes because the past cannot be changed and lessons have to be learned.

> *Self-reflection will help to identify where mistakes were made, how to avoid repeating them and where improvements can be made in the future.*

The focus should be on both failures and successes, as these may both be helpful when identifying ways to improve the overall performance of the individual and the team.

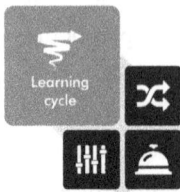

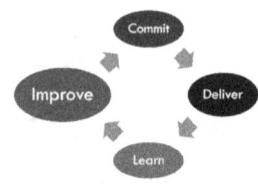

Commit

Improve

Deliver

Learn

IMPROVE

A quick win for improvement is expanding on learnings so far: do better or more of what worked well, do differently or less of what did not work. Thereafter the focus should be on the phase of the engagement process where the most improvement can be expected. If improvements in the three stages of engagement are no longer creating better results, the overall focus has to change.

What improvement is likely to create most impact?

Preparation → All relevant information, knowledge, goals and approach available before engagement

Execution → Connecting, understanding, updating and closing were all executed well

Follow-up → Confirmation, progress tracking, updating and delivery all went well

Focus/choice → Make changes in contact person, preferred solution, type of engagement, or decide to move on

MANAGEMENT
MASTER MIND

CHAPTER 13

IMPROVE

*'An error doesn't become a mistake
until you refuse to correct it.'*

ORLANDO BATTISTA

The final step in the learning cycle is aimed at addressing the root causes for either over- or under-performances that were identified during the learning phase as described in the previous chapter.

> *In this final step, after identifying those areas that need to be improved, less effective actions can be adjusted to improve results.*

Result goals should not be changed during the week, but changes to action improvements are acceptable where the expectation is that the new actions will create a higher likelihood of achieving those committed result goals. If, for example, 'doing things better', is really not working well, then of course the action should be shifted to 'doing things differently'. It is an employee's responsibility to take ownership for their own development and to continuously find ways to **improve** their actions. They should be encouraged and motivated in this respect, although changing action goals should preferably be done in agreement with the manager so that the manager knows what to expect when inspecting what is expected.

The football coach watching the game does not always wait for half time to engage with players on what improvements could be made. This also applies to the working environment where:

> **There is no need to wait for formal engagement to start implementing changes that seem to make sense.**

The reason for trying an enhanced approach during the same week is to examine whether the preliminary understanding of the root causes, based on analysis so far, was correct. Once the outcome of this new approach has shown the expected improvement, the new activity becomes known as a best practice. All the new best practices learned should be shared with the whole team at the end of the week's debriefing session so that colleagues can learn from the experience of their peers. Sharing all the lessons learned with the whole team at the end of the week helps to fast-track the building up of experiences, creates a positive team spirit, and can also boost team performance.

HOW TO IMPROVE

If the results of a task failed to meet expectations, the action improvements in this final step of the learning cycle are likely to require that tasks be performed in a better or different way. However, if the actions proved to be successful, any improvements can be made by doing more of the same. Doing more of something may require making time for this additional activity by doing less of something else. More, better, different or less can be applied to many areas, depending on the outcome of the analysis. Although different approaches could be applied to find areas for improvement, a good starting point would be to zoom in on the weakest link in the four steps of execution. The following examples show what the improvement could look like:

- **Was the root cause related to poor *preparation*?**

  Do research and gather more relevant information about the engagement partner.

  Improve any knowledge about what the organisation has to offer.

  Gain a better understanding of what should be achieved during the engagement.

  Be prepared to come up with other options when responding to objections.

- **Was the root cause related to poor *execution*?**

  Spend more time getting to know customers and engagement partners.

  Gain a better understanding of what is most relevant for the customer.

  Do more checks in order to manage customers' expectations.

  Ensure more clarity on what will happen after the meeting.

- **Was the root cause related to poor *follow-up*?**

  Ensure quicker confirmation to customers by email on what was agreed during the meeting.

  Keep a better record of progress made.

  Have more regular engagements in order to keep updating what will happen next.

  Find out at delivery whether the customer is fully satisfied with the outcome.

- **Or, is there a need to change *focus*?**

  If the contact person has no mandate for decision making, find a person with a higher authority who does.

  Find alternative solutions that better suit the customer's needs. Change the setting to a lunch venue, for example.

Reach a consensus that proceeding with the task may not be in the person's or company's best interest.

These are all suggestions for improvements, but for different root causes. Where employees are not able to identify any areas of improvement for themselves, the manager can simply ask some of these questions as a way to encourage them to finding their own solutions.

EMBEDDING IMPROVEMENT

Improvements made during the week will be either successful or unsuccessful. Regardless of the outcome, everyone on the team should be able to provide a summary during the end-of-week debrief on the things they have learned and what the results were. For example:

- 'I committed myself to call ten prospects to set up five meetings for next week ...'
  (Referring to the commitment made during the action improvement meeting.)

- 'What worked well is that I reached all prospects that I tried to call just before lunch, and what did not work well is that I only managed to arrange three meetings for next week.'
  (Referring to the actions and outcome.)

- 'What I learned from this was that prospects are interested, but bigger companies have a budget cycle and they do not like to meet when it has not been budgeted for.'
  (Referring to the root cause analysis, which highlighted an understanding of areas needing improvement.)

- 'Therefore, I changed my approach, and as a result I will make sure that I will allocate more time for meetings and workshop in August/ September each year to make presentations when prospects are working on their budget proposals. We will prepare our proposals such that finance departments can quickly assess the business case and expected return on investment.'

  (Explaining what the biggest lessons learned were and how challenges were overcome.)

Lessons learned and best practices should be translated into improvements in the next learning cycle with new stretching assignments, otherwise employees will lose motivation and their enthusiasm will decrease. The goal is not only to improve results, but also to groom employees to become better and climb the career ladder. New commitments should be specific and require continuous care and control from the manager.

> **The learning cycle step of 'Improve' is to help employees break the habit of 'doing what you always did'.**

The purpose of implementing small changes on a weekly basis is to ensure employees continue learning and developing their skills in a way that poses little risk to them or the organisation, and will ensure results are achieved quickly and effectively. Employees who are already performing well are challenged to explore ways of improving even further. Organisations that are successful run the risk of becoming complacent and allowing their competitors to catch up with them. For this reason, no organisation can ever afford to stagnate, and all employees and managers need to continually explore opportunities and keep up to date with the market developments.

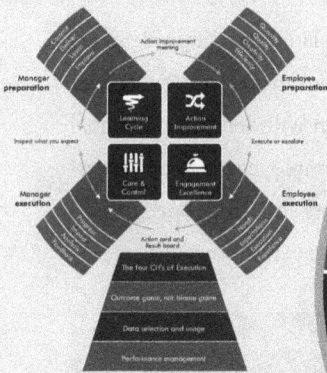

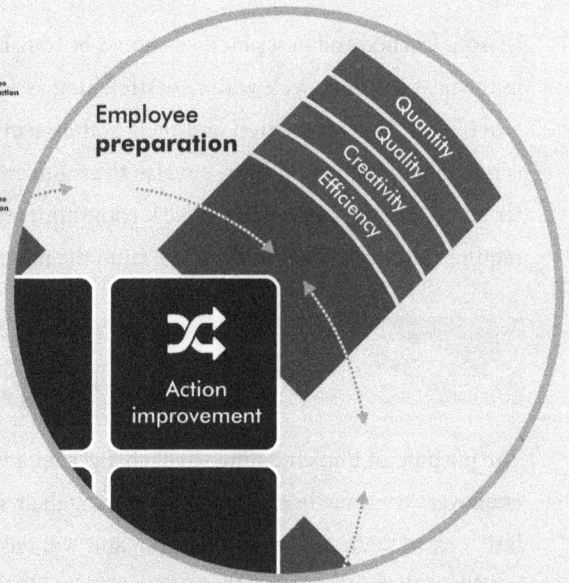

PART 4:

ACTION IMPROVEMENT

The next blade in the MILL model is **action improvement**.

This is where the lessons learned in the learning cycle are put into practice by adjusting behaviour.

This means that employees and managers commit to doing **more** of something, doing something **better**, doing something **differently**, or doing something **less** in order to work towards becoming an LHPO.

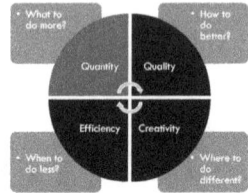

QUANTITY → MORE

If a certain action creates results, doing it more will create more results. More can also be applicable in terms of applying the same approach in other circumstances. More implies that there is always a number to improve, which makes 'more' easy to manage. This number game is often the quickest way to create success.

More often → The frequency of actions, how many times, more outcome

More time → Stage of engagement where time-squeeze has an impact on result

More extended → Multiple options will make it easier to choose

More focus → Low effort/high impact (quick wins could create more momentum for success)

MANAGEMENT
MASTER MIND

CHAPTER 14

MORE

'It aint' about how hard you can hit, it's about how hard you
can get hit and keep moving forward.'

ROCKY BALBOA

The first action improvement, or behavioural change, that we will look at is about what can be done more.

> *It is based upon an understanding of which actions worked well, and assumes that doing more of the same will also lead to more results.*

Do not change the winning team, but challenge them do more, to win more and to stay in the lead. The challenge with the action improvement of doing things more is that employees are already 'winning' or, in other words, they are already successful. As a result, they may feel that there is no necessity or reason to change. The manager should appreciate the good results and still encourage employees to perform these tasks more frequently, more consistently and with more discipline. A football team that is in the lead by 3–0 at half time could slow down in the second half or could aim for 6–0 in the second half. Which of these two options will create more excitement, more confidence and more pride among players and fans? Stretching for more is always better than becoming complacent.

THE MANAGER'S ROLE

The manager's role is to ensure there is sufficient clarity on whatever action can and will be performed more, based on the ideas generated and selected by the employees. When setting goals during the action improvement meetings, the manager should try to stretch the initial commitment made by the employee to aim for more in both their action and result goals, as some employees may be conservative and prefer to remain in their comfort zone.

> *If they aren't stretched, employees may stagnate, remain in the safe zone and not experience development and growth.*

If an employee says, 'I will do it three times a day,' the manager should ask, 'Why not five times?' If the employee is still fine with five times, then the manager should challenge them further and ask, 'And what about seven times?'

> *When targets are set on the high side, employees automatically realise that more thought has to be given on proper preparation and thorough planning.*

Preparation for an exam will be postponed if the topic is perceived to be easy. But if a student has to write a dissertation, which is obviously difficult, their preparation is likely to begin earlier and be better. It is very human to procrastinate, expecting that tomorrow is a better day, and therefore the manager has to put some pressure on employees by inspecting what is expected and encouraging employees to get things over and done with. This will help them to feel encouraged and more enthusiastic about continuing with their assignment. Without this encouragement, employees will fill their time with unnecessary tasks to avoid the more complicated tasks they were supposed to do. Job satisfaction will increase when staff feel that they had a productive day, doing important tasks recognised by the manager.

Employees will never 'get the time' that they are hoping for to pick up stretching action improvements; therefore, the manager has to guide the process of the employees 'making time' for more activities that will stretch them. The employee should be allowed to take responsibility to manage their own time, as long as they don't blame others when a task is not completed on time. Employees have to be challenged to specify which less important tasks can be postponed without consequence, or can be done less frequently or quicker in order to create time for important tasks.

A manager's tone of voice is crucial in terms of how they challenge employees to do more. If employees are pushed too hard, it may create the impression that the manager only has an interest in seeing them working harder. Instead, the manager should let their employees know that it is also in their interests to be doing more, because they will achieve better results or will learn more.

> **The goal is to stretch them so that they experience development, not stress them.**

When an employee has very little self-confidence, stretching them can make them become stressed more quickly than an employee who is self-confident. The manager needs to take small steps when stretching a less confident employee. By acknowledging their first successful achievement at an early stage, the manager will help the employee to grow in confidence as tasks become more difficult.

THE EMPLOYEE'S ROLE

Applying the action improvement of performing actions more is based on analysis showing that employees are on the right track and doing the right things. There is no need to do something better, differently or less. Simply spending more time on something, or putting more effort into doing the same thing is expected to increase the results. Improvements from doing something more can apply to both activities performed as preparation or follow-up, or activities performed during the engagement. Following are two examples of what can be done more before and after engagements, and two examples of what can be done more during the engagement.

- **More preparation**

  More preparation can be done by envisioning what the expected outcome of the engagement *could* be (preparing more options, so having a plan B and plan C) or *should* be (more focus on the outcome, so remember to ask for commitment). In order to have a more constructive meeting, there needs to be more clarity on what both the employee's and also the engagement partner's expectations are. This also implies that more information needs to be collated about the engagement partner prior to the engagement itself.

- **More follow-up**

  An excellent way of managing an engagement partner's expectations and keeping them in the loop is to do a proper follow-up with them. This involves sharing what progress has been made and what the next steps are. When more frequent follow-up takes place and more details are provided about what can be expected, there is more likelihood of a successful outcome. Follow-up is key when building and maintaining relationships. Personal contacts are, most of the time, better appreciated than the perfect solution, and therefore follow-up is key to building and maintaining relationships when the product/solution itself may not be that much different from your competitors.

- **More understanding**

  A proper understanding of the engagement partner is often blurred by our own perceptions. We tend to look for similarities in what the other person's preferences are, and even in what they feel to be important. The solution for avoiding this pitfall is to continually ask more questions about what is important to them to try to understand the environment in which they operate, and how considerations and decisions are made.

- **More options**

  In order to find the best solution, it can be productive to discuss more options in terms of possible deliveries or of what will happen next. Pre-empting different scenarios is a helpful way of understanding what really is important to the engagement partner, and also whether there are other competitive options they may consider. They may already have an idea of what they are looking for and, as such, having more discussions on various alternatives can reveal better options.

Things that can be done more – more calls, more visits, more options – can often be implemented quickly.

> *The action improvement of more is, however, not only about working harder but also about consistency and discipline. In other words, doing what needs to be done, in the right way, again and again.*

While stretching employees to do more, there should be sufficient attention to avoid quality being jeopardised. The action improvement itself is not the goal: the ultimate goal is increasing bottom line results, the quality and innovation strength of the company, as well as what employees can learn and achieve. Therefore a balanced approach is required to achieve sustainable growth.

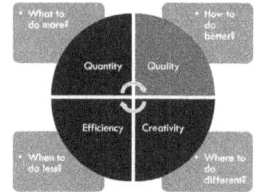

QUALITY → BETTER

Improving quality may be considered if efforts for quantity improvement (more) are showing limited impact. A different approach is to first improve the quality and only scale up to doing things more once a good formula has been found.

Quality improvements of engagement:

- Preparation, execution, follow-up

Quality improvement of personal skills:

- Listening, capturing information, understanding, responding

Quality improvement of facilitation:

- Proposition, clarification/communication, tracking, internal support

Quality improvement of attitude:

- -Non-verbal communication, eagerness, ownership, belief, ambition

MANAGEMENT
MASTER MIND

CHAPTER 15

BETTER

'The bitterness of poor quality remains long after the sweetness of low price is forgotten.'

BENJAMIN FRANKLIN

The second action improvement is about doing things better. This is about the quality of work. The quest for quality improvement has become more important nowadays, as the internet provides global access to both knowledge and products and customers are more informed as well as more demanding.

> **Employees should take ownership of quality and pay more attention to the details when growing the organisation from good to great.**

Even the smallest mistake can have an enormous impact in a highly competitive market, and a good reputation can quickly be destroyed should just one customer make a negative comment via social media.

Quality assurance is a well-known concept in the production and information technology sectors, but similar notions can be utilised in other areas of business. Doing work right the first time is a key concept for many production companies – it involves trying to do better by avoiding having to make corrections – but this same principle can also be embedded in many other types of organisations. An alternative for doing things right the first time is the setting up of a one-stop shopping concept, which means that all needs and all cross-selling opportunities are explored during one meeting.

THE MANAGER'S ROLE

There are a number of reasons why a manager should include 'doing things better' on the agenda for the action improvement meeting.

- In cases of negative performance trends, increasing costs, high numbers of complaints, poor customer ratings and so forth, the focus should be on doing things better. The challenge is not to find reasons to blame somebody for problems, but rather ask employees to take ownership for solutions by exploring opportunities and potential ways to become better.

> *The goal should not be to lower the number of existing complaints – this is more about avoidance than improvement – but to see what can be done better to increase the number of satisfied customers.*

- The focus during action improvement meetings could also alternate between doing things in a better way during one week and doing things more in the other week.

> *Doing things more may have negative effects on quality, and therefore this approach should be balanced with doing things better for maintaining sustainable growth.*

Organisations that have very limited resources, or are new in a particular market, may even want to begin by initially focusing on quality. Scaling up by doing things more will only make sense once a good working formula has been established. Some organisations may have split responsibilities, for example the sales department (front office) may be focused on bringing in more business, while the administrative department (back office) focuses more on quality. Under the MILL model, the intention is for quantity and quality to go hand-in-hand. Managers must ensure departments work together as teams on sustainable growth, and find the balance between doing things more and doing things better.

- The manager is also encouraged to review their own role in the various process steps of the MILL model in order to identify where action improvements of doing things better can be made. Implementing the model has to be done in phases, and the manager should continuously practise this to become better. The manager should also conduct an evaluation of what worked well and what did not work well and then go on to make appropriate changes. Any new approach to be explored must be communicated to employees to get their buy-in and relevant feedback. This will also show that the manager is leading by example, in terms of personal development, by practising and continuously searching for self-improvement. Explaining what will be done better and why will make employees appreciate the change more than if they're surprised by new behaviour by the manager, which can make employees suspicious and wonder what's going on.

THE EMPLOYEE'S ROLE

When an employee is trying to achieve a better quality outcome, it is not about performing a task as quickly as possible, but about putting in best efforts and performing to the best of their capabilities. Below are some examples of what can be done better in order to achieve an improved outcome during the engagement process.

- **Better organisation**

  Where there is no proper organisation and insufficient planning of work, people generally prefer to complete the easiest tasks first and leave the more complex ones for later. It is therefore essential to allocate time at the end of each day to plan the next day's events. Important and complex tasks require more planning and should therefore be given priority. Beware of trying to accommodate urgent tasks triggered by someone else's lack of planning. Employees will stop planning if the manager keeps coming up with ad-hoc 'urgent' tasks, which makes it seem as if making a plan does not make sense.

> *The notion that 'If you cannot plan, I cannot plan' can spread quickly and will make an organisation responsive only to emergencies.*

Using a tracking tool is highly beneficial. It helps to trace the progress of tasks or projects while dealing with them, and helps to maintain professional working relationships with customers by ensuring that follow-up is better. Employees tend to focus their attentions more on acquisitions instead of on the retention of existing customers, but doing better in retaining customers is proven to have a higher payoff for any effort put into a project.

Working better can also be done by developing templates for meeting confirmations, offerings, checklists and other recurring documents. To explore the added value of tools, the action improvement meeting can focus on generating ideas for tools to make the engagement process more effective (internally) or more professional (externally).

- **Better teamwork**

  When working as part of a team, it is essential to have regular team-building sessions in order to strengthen team spirit. Stretching a team could result in some tensions among team members because they all have their unique strengths and weaknesses. It is recommended that, to address potential differences or tensions, teams should conduct monthly meetings in order to maintain mutual support, cooperation, specialisation and knowledge exchange. During such dedicated meetings, team members will agree on where improvements can be made in order for them to work better and more effectively as a team. Team building is not something that you only have to do once a year – by jumping on mountain bikes or climbing a wall together – but should be business-as-usual in the normal working environment in order to evaluate the team performance. Teams can show stronger performance than the individuals' combined performance when individual members realise that the team's success is their success.

- **Better use of the N(EX)3 approach**

  We have already discussed the N(EX)3 approach and its advantages (refer to Chapter 2), but employees should consider refining the way they use it as a way of doing things better. First let's review the skills that can be utilised during an engagement, which are related to:

a) Recognising need-signals in order to know what solution to offer for different situations.

b) Capturing relevant information, such as marital status for recommendations on insurance.

c) Understanding the reason why customers have ambitions or fears, as these may differ from one's own and therefore require empathy to find the best solution.

d) Responding in a way that is in line with the customers' expectations.

The generic skill set that is required to see what can be done better is related to listening, questioning, summarising and explaining.

It is recommended to practise these skills by simulating more challenging customer engagement situations and allowing people to try a better approach in a safe environment among colleagues. It is also recommended that teams get into pairs on a regular basis during engagements, to provide each other with mutually beneficial and constructive feedback on areas where improvements can be made.

- **Better attention to detail**
  Action improvements focusing on quality can be very powerful, because even the smallest improvement can make a big difference to the outcome of the engagement. The key for exceeding customer expectations is to gain an excellent understanding of what is important to customers, and therefore be able to make improvements in terms of

preparation, execution and follow-up. People can often be 'penny-wise and pound-foolish', and the new science of behavioural economics also proves that customers do not always think or act logically. By conducting proper and professional engagements with customers, and by being aware of the smallest details, the answers to many questions will be provided. You will understand what matters most to customers, and therefore what can be done more effectively, or in a better way, to achieve a better outcome.

Unlike the action improvement of doing things more, the action improvement of doing things better requires better analysis and research, and the generation of multiple ideas. It can, however, be very rewarding when small improvements have a big impact on quality; repeatedly performing slightly better than competitors will in itself generate success. No matter how insignificant they may seem, the little things are important to customers. For example, remembering birthdays and even hobbies, or sending a handwritten note thanking them for their business, or forwarding articles which may be of interest to them. These are all small acts, but well worth the effort of following through, as they will go a long way towards creating lasting and successful business relationships. Doing things better, even small things, can have a big impact.

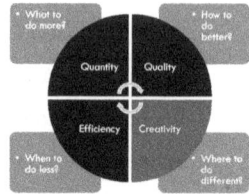

CREATIVITY→DIFFERENT

The principles for improvement follow the rule that the most difficult path is probably also the most rewarding path. Doing something different may require more time, broader thinking outside the sector and more experimenting. Creativity should always be appreciated and unconventional thinking encouraged.

Different/creativity in the how of engagement:
➜ The tools used, the setting, the wording, etc.

Different/creativity in the what of engagement:
➜ The frequency, the focus, the speed of follow-up, etc.

Different/creativity in the marketing Ps:
➜ Changes in pricing, promotion, product or distribution

Different/creativity in relationship management➜ Type of follow-up, survey on satisfaction, ways to show appreciation, etc.

CHAPTER 16:

DIFFERENT

'In order to be content men must also have the possibility of developing their intellectual and artistic powers.'

ALBERT EINSTEIN

The third action improvement is about doing things **differently**. In other words, it's about creativity.

> **When the previous action improvements of doing things more or better no longer improve results, it may be time to consider what could be done differently.**

It can be very refreshing to challenge staff to come up with new ideas on how the team can work smarter instead of harder. At the same time, however, doing things differently could be perceived as being somewhat threatening, as one cannot build on experience and there may be uncertainty about the response and outcome of new initiatives.

This is one of the key reasons why successful companies can, over a period of time, lose their strong position in the market. If senior management achieved their positions based on historical knowledge and experience, they may feel threatened by new employees who have more innovative ideas. This means that these future leaders may face resistance and rejection from the 'establishment'. Organisations that have a tendency to promote the most knowledgeable employees and encourage them to climb the ladder may have this challenge even more deeply entrenched.

> **Managers should realise that their main responsibility is not to know more or have more experience, but rather to get the very best out of their subordinates.**

This section explains in more depth how innovation in an organisation can be embraced and stimulated, and how to adapt and keep up with a continuously changing environment.

THE BENEFITS OF INNOVATION

When challenged to come up with innovative and new ideas on what can be performed differently, employees should be encouraged to conduct research in different sectors outside the company. This will help them become aware of external developments, and of potential opportunities and threats. When management makes decisions that more drastic innovations are to be implemented, employees will already have a much better understanding of the need for change as well as the opportunities that may be generated.

Employees should then be gradually exposed to changes that are about to be implemented. Encouraging employees to be more innovative will motivate them to be less resistant to change. By involving employees in the early stages of innovation, opportunities will also be provided for their own ideas and concerns to be incorporated. If employees take ownership of finding innovation, they will be more likely to be proactive and show enthusiasm to prove the success of their ideas.

Involving employees from the beginning also allows small steps in the development to be tested in the market, which provides feedback to the developers. By gradual and partial implementation of innovations, further improvements can be made based on market-related insights while still continuing with the development. This allows the MILL model focus on action learning to be incorporated in the innovation process.

THE MANAGER'S ROLE

In order to fully explore the potential of employees to come up with their own ideas on what can be done differently, management also has to consider engaging with them in a different manner. There is a tendency for managers to discount or ignore potential ideas coming from new employees that question or challenge an existing way of working. Instead of embracing these new insights and appreciating the diversity of a team, the existing employees may feel threatened if the new employees criticise the way they work.

Instead, managers could, for example, ask newly employed employees to keep track of any observations and suggestions they have during the first two or three months of their employment using lessons learned in other organisations. These insights should be used as input for the action improvement meeting when discussing options for what can be done differently.

There will always be reasons why an idea may not work in its entirety; therefore, a manager should avoid discussions about whether the idea, as a whole, could be beneficial. Instead, employees could be challenged to decide which elements of the idea or approach can be utilised and enhanced further for the benefit of the organisation.

The intention should be for experienced employees to be teamed up with new employees for mutual learning. Teams are much stronger when each member is willing to exchange information, and to learn from the others by applying mutual support and constructive feedback.

THE EMPLOYEE'S ROLE

It is not common for management to engage with individual employees in terms of how they plan and organise their daily work. It could, however, be useful to set up an action improvement meeting to give employees an opportunity to share individual best practices on how to organise their work and learn what can be done differently. Below are two examples of common challenges that may need to be approached differently.

- **Time tracking**
  Creating an awareness of how time is spent is the first step towards understanding what can be done differently in order to manage time better. A helpful way to determine whether time is being spent efficiently is to ask employees what their top five priorities are and how much time, on average, they spend on each of them per week. It is quite common to find that less than sixty per cent of weekly hours can be accounted for, while the remaining time is much less productive because of distractions caused by the internet, social talk or other disruptions.

Employees, however, may feel overwhelmed by their duties and how much they are expected to do. These feelings of being overwhelmed are generally caused by all kinds of small, unimportant and less structured activities considered to be 'time wasters'; that is, interruptions and emails. In order to address this challenge, an action improvement meeting can be conducted to agree on what could be done differently in terms of timing, approach, the tools used and the time spent on daily recurring activities.

- **Different support/tools**

  If not well-coordinated, interactions between departments and their support departments can be very challenging and have a big impact on productivity and staff morale. Employees do not feel encouraged to give their best if they do not get proper support from other departments, or if they are not aware of limitations and challenges in these other departments. To create better interdepartmental teamwork, joint action improvement meetings can be held between the support and the receiving departments. An improved mutual understanding of work completed and the daily challenges and frustrations of each cooperating department can help address problems by agreeing on how to work differently and more effectively as a team.

DOING THINGS DIFFERENTLY DURING ENGAGEMENT

If calling more customers does not appear to add value, or if having a better script when calling is not improving responses, then it may be time to try something different. It might, for example, be worth trying to organise a breakfast meeting or a seminar with well-known speakers to find out whether a new kind of engagement would have a more successful impact. There are multiple options for reviewing the current approach. Below are two examples of possible ways of trying a different approach.

- **Interact differently**

  The way employees apply customer engagement may become routine and tedious – for both employees and customers – when the same process is consistently followed over time. A different and more creative approach could be refreshing without jeopardising minimal requirements. For example, passenger safety demonstrations on commercial airline flights have become more entertaining and less formal, and therefore draw more attention. It is always beneficial to be aware of how other sectors carry out engagements with their customers and to see what elements can be duplicated. In the hospitality sector, for example, restaurants have begun to serve similar food in more creative ways, such as presenting it in baskets, or on flat stones or wooden boards. Creativity can also be applied within an organisation by conducting meetings in which employees stand up instead of sitting down. The goal is to come up with creative ideas for action improvement by introducing different experiences.

- **Focus differently**

  When an employee repeatedly uses the same approach during engagements with customers, it can be very refreshing to try a different approach and see how another colleague (or colleagues) would act in the same situation. When colleagues work together, they are able to learn valuable skills from each other as well as provide constructive feedback. Both employees should be encouraged to agree that, after every exchange, they will try at least one insight they have learned from the other to see whether something different will also work for them. It may, for example, add more value if the employee asks different questions, listens more or talks less. Depending on the engagement, a PowerPoint presentation may not be the right approach, but conducting a short survey may provide more relevant customer insights to help improve the quality of engagement.

The third action improvement of doing things different is about being more creative and focusing on doing things differently.

Creativity in employees should be encouraged and nurtured as an unconventional way of thinking that opens new doors. Finding these areas of untapped market potential may require some trial and error but, once found, the results can be very rewarding.

Where employees feel forced into making changes by doing things differently before they are ready to, there will be a certain amount of resistance. But:

> *When employees are challenged in a positive way to initiate change and their input is taken seriously, they will be more likely to buy in to making necessary changes.*

Exploring what can be done differently using the MILL model will, therefore, facilitate quicker and better implementation of innovation and change.

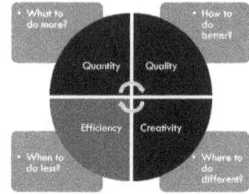

EFFICIENCY → LESS/STOP

There will never be time to do more, better or different unless you make time. So either start with identifying where time can be saved or schedule a clean-up of time-wasting activities every now and then. It is important to quantify time that is expected to be saved and fill this space immediately with important activities (other action improvements). Without doing this, freed-up time may still be wasted.

Efficiency of meetings: poor upfront information sharing, not focused on guidance, decision making or action tracking, poor time management

Efficiency of time management: low-value activities, limited strategic importance activities, poor planning

Efficiency of support: support also focused on engagement excellence, self-monitoring by support department, service level agreements

Efficiency by management: clear alignment with overall goals, split priorities into Priority 1/2/3, support for making time

MANAGEMENT
MASTER MIND

CHAPTER 17

LESS

'Work expands so as to fill the time available for its completion.'

CYRIL NORTHCOTE PARKINSON

The final building block of action improvement is about efficiency and, in order to be more efficient, the most time consuming and most frequent tasks must be evaluated to determine if they can be performed **less** often, or even **stopped**. Where there are time constraints in executing the previous three action improvements (doing something **more**, **better** or **differently**) it may be necessary to first organise an action improvement meeting to focus on ways to become more efficient.

> *When additional time is created as a result of an action improvement meeting focused on what can be done less, it is important to know, from the beginning, how to use this freed up time efficiently.*

If this is not the case, employees may use the extra time to pick up new menial tasks or take more time for existing, low added-value activities. Understanding how the time that was 'created' can be allocated effectively will go a long way towards helping employees to be more focused on planning, as well as on how they manage their time. The intention is ultimately for the entire team to postpone or cancel less important activities.

To create focus and get a cumbersome assignment/ challenge out of the way, it could make sense to agree with the entire team to all work on that same task at the same time from the same space.

> **The team should be encouraged to have one shared activity to work on daily.**

For example, the team could work shoulder-to shoulder on a certain activity every morning, until lunch time, in order to address challenging tasks. It can be very stimulating for the team spirit to have all team members perform the same activities at the same time and, preferably, even from the same place (in sales this is called a 'war room'). All that is required to create this team effort is for the manager to provide support for employees' proposals about which other activities can be parked or postponed, thus allowing the team to focus on the important ones. If there is synergy between members of the team, they will be more successful as they focus on and prioritise more important tasks.

COMMON INEFFICIENCIES

Allowing employees to come up with ideas on where time can be saved is very motivating. Without allowing this, stretching them in other areas (more, better, different) could cause some friction. In each instance, dedicated action improvement meetings can be held to discuss and determine which actions can be performed less or stopped altogether in order to save time or even improve performance. Below are four areas where time can be saved, as well as suggested ways to change practices for the better:

- **Cumbersome processes**

  Sometimes processes can become cumbersome, and process re-engineering can be explored by employees with the right skills to see what can be done less in order to be more effective. A goal, for example, could be to see how the number of people involved in one task can be reduced. Every time a document is shifted to another desk or 'in tray' it causes a delay. There should be no need for the same action to be repeated unnecessarily during the same process. So, if one document requires input from four different employees, but also requires signatures from three more, this is likely not the most efficient way of undertaking a task – especially when none of the employees providing input or needing to sign the document are directly involved in the overall process. The more action-owners there are and the more steps there are that have to be followed, the more time consuming a process becomes and the more likely it is to cause delays.

It is also recommended that fixed timeslots are created for batch processing. Activities that are continuously started and stopped, with employees hopping from one task to another, create a very inefficient use of time. During each step in a process, it is worth asking any of the following questions:

- Is this step really adding value?
- Can the step be delegated to someone else on the team?
- Can the step be automated?
- Can the step be centralised to a specialised department?
- Is it worth outsourcing this step?

- **Ineffective meetings**

  The goal of a meeting must be made clear to all attendees, and its purpose may even need to be repeated frequently to ensure all participants take responsibility for having a time-efficient and effective meeting. Information should be shared in good time *before* meetings, not just *during* the meeting. This gives participants time to prepare for the meeting by reading through the relevant information. If meetings are not used for exchanging best practices and no new commitments are being made, then the time will be wasted.

  In order for meetings to run well, the focus should be on the following:

  - Feedback: observation and qualification.
    'What we like/dislike so far is ... while the following issues are the most serious ...'

  - Guidance: redirecting and stretching.
    'What we expect to see in the next meeting is more/better/different/less ...'

  - Decision making: proposals and non-negotiables.
    'We agree on the following very specific decisions or assignments ...'

  - Action commitment: action and result goals.
    'These are the actions that can be expected after the meeting ... that aim for the following result ...'

  Often, by the end of meetings, the decisions and commitment are still disappointing and very little has been achieved. Participants easily become complacent and assume results will improve by the time the next meeting is held. This is because no clarity has been provided on why, how or even what the new action commitments should be, or how they could be improved.

> **When meetings are held without implementing suggested changes for improvements or addressing any of the four focus points, they will continue to be ineffective and a waste of valuable time.**

Participants will stop preparing for them and stop actioning the outcome.

- **Reporting overload**

  When employees are empowered and delegated to complete a task, they have a duty to keep track of what they are doing as part of the trust implied by this process. The manager allows the employees to act more independently, but they still have overall responsibility and therefore some tracking and reporting is required. Reporting should, however, be limited to analysis and actions initiated by employees.

  Instead of expecting that employees will collect data from the systems and making data reports for management so that management can do the analysis and recommendations, the MILL model suggests that it should be the other way around. Management should instruct IT/Finance to make data available in an easily accessible format (a 'dashboard'). Thereafter, the employees can use this dashboard for their own analysis and personal recommendations, and these proposals for action will be used to report to management for their vetting and endorsement.

  This is better for data integrity and also allows more time for the employee to focus on analysis and action improvements. Reports made by staff should also always receive some feedback. If there is no feedback, the employee may not understand what the recipient is doing with the report and/or may feel that there is no care. In both cases, the making of reports will quickly become a nuisance.

REPORTING OVERLOAD

1. Employee is asked to collect and supply data

2. Manager analyses results so far

3. Manager instructs what should be done

4. Manager checks whether actions are successful

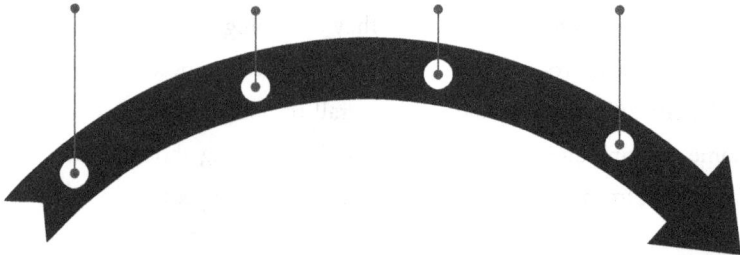

WHO IS IN THE DRIVING SEAT ?

The employee is NOT in the Driving Seat but waits for instruction and guidance!!
Ownership and empowerment go down.

1. Manager supplies a Dashboard showing successes- and shortfalls

2. Employee is asked to assess root-cause and develop action improvement

3. Manager will check analysis, actions and results for guidance and leadership assessment

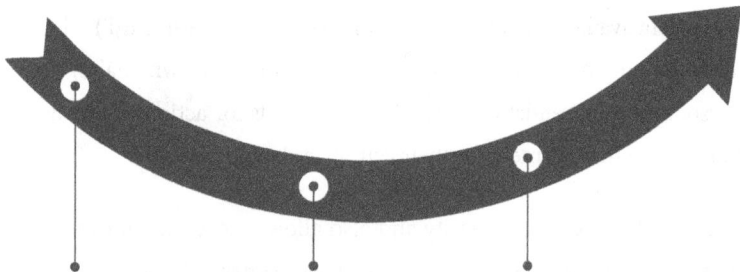

The employee is in the Driving Seat (for a learning organization)!!
Ownership and empowerment go up.

- **Poor support**

  Employees must be allowed to remain focused on their primary duties, and they should also be able to rely on support from managers when they need it. This allows employees to fully utilise their skills and allows employers to get the best out of them.

> *To create alignment and teamwork, the support departments should share the same key tools and guiding principles so that the whole organisation speaks the same language.*

There should be service levels in place that help to clarify what is expected of employees in terms of internal support. Here are four examples of what should be addressed in a service level agreement:

1. **Proactive support:** Support departments (any department that does not have an external customer engagement is, in fact, supportive to the business departments) are supposed to take the initiative and research where either more, better or different support can be offered. Ideas can be collected by conducting action improvement meetings.

2. **Service orientation:** Support departments will act on the needs of the business departments instead of imposing their own priorities and rules. Working relationships with internal customers need to be taken seriously by utilising engagement excellence principles. These will be explained in the next part of the book.

3. **Management of expectations:** Support departments should always clarify what the next steps are and should manage expectations by ensuring timelines are managed. Explaining dependencies and the added value of time-consuming process steps will help to create a better understanding of timelines.

4. **Self-monitoring:** Support departments are expected to have their own tracking processes in place so that delays can be communicated and challenges escalated in a timely manner. There should be no need for the receiving department to send reminders or queries once the delivering department has committed.

Normally, the action improvement meeting will only allow for ideas that can be implemented immediately, but this cannot be expected from interdepartmental action improvement meetings as some broader decision making and endorsements may be required before implementation can commence.

THE EMPLOYEE'S ROLE

Employees can drive efficiency improvements by researching, for themselves, how to become more efficient in the following four areas:

- **Planning**

  The most effective way of managing time is through proper planning. The more time we are given to do something, the longer it will take to complete – this is normal human behaviour. Often, despite being given an assignment months in advance, we often wait until the very last minute before any serious preparation is done.

> *In order to work efficiently, big tasks can be broken down into smaller sections, which means that less effort will be required to complete the task.*

- **Back-ups**

  When important issues are given focused time, they will not become urgent.

> *Where 'urgencies' are a part of the business, allocating an open timeslot for potential urgencies will prevent them from becoming disruptive.*

Also when no time is allocated for important tasks, there will never be excess time suddenly available, to complete them. Always schedule a provisional back-up meeting so that important meetings are not missed altogether if they have to be rescheduled due to unforeseen circumstances. This allows for continuity in the decision-making process, which keeps the momentum up and spirits high. Cancelling meetings could be perceived as a sign of disrespect for or non-interest in the agenda of the meeting.

- **Batch processing**

  Avoid distracting activities such as checking emails every five minutes, as they are very time consuming. It is more beneficial to schedule limited but dedicated time to perform ad-hoc tasks like emails. Schedule them for the end of the day or just before lunchtime, for example.

By regularly focusing on what can be done less, time can be freed up to perform the other action improvements to do something more, better or differently. It is up to both managers and employees to regularly find ways to streamline the running of the organisation to ensure efficiency and to stay focused.

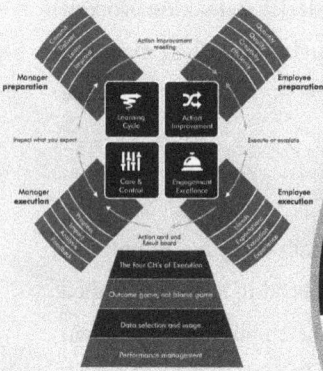

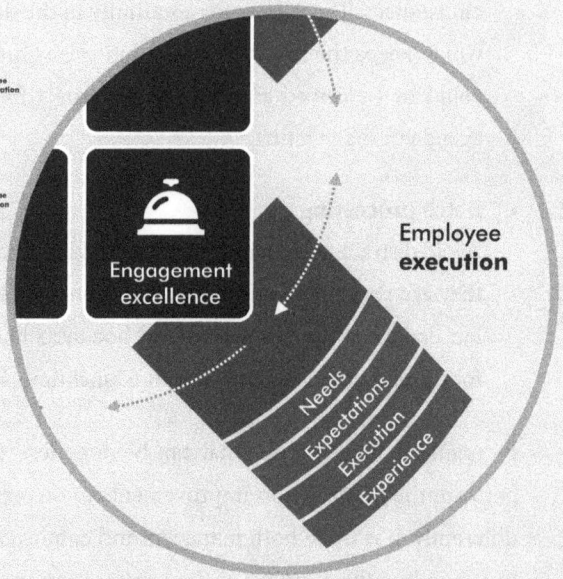

PART 5:
ENGAGEMENT EXCELLENCE

The next blade of the MILL model is **engagement excellence**. This part of the book refers to both internal engagements between colleagues and external engagements held with customers. Because internal engagement is about teaming up and supporting each other, this book will refer to colleagues as 'conversation partners' when referring to engagement within the organisation. Whether internal or external, to achieve engagement excellence the goal remains the same. It is to maximise added value for either the external customer or the internal conversation partner. The next four chapters will describe all the four N(EX)3 building blocks of engagement excellence in more detail. As a reminder, N(EX)3 stands for:

- **(N)** Understanding **Needs**
- **(EX)** Updating **Expectations**
- **(EX)** Committing to **Execution**
- **(EX)** Checking the **Experience**

Engagement excellence

Understand/ Needs → Update/ Expectation → Undertake/ Execution → Up to satisfaction/ Experience

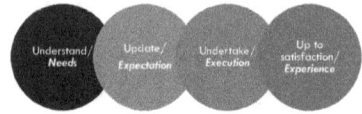

NEEDS → UNDERSTAND

The starting point of any engagement is to get a sense of what the engagement partner tries to achieve. How will the future state look like and what added value is expected from this engagement? Customers may already have an idea of the product/solution they are looking for, but only by asking beyond the obvious will it become clear where the offering can differ from competitors to achieve engagement excellence.

Future state

- What will change after needs are fulfilled? (more factual)

Future emotion

- Why is this important to you? (more emotional)

Executing difference

- What will be most appreciated in the deliverable? (ranking priority)

Engagement expectation

- Any other specific request or expectation on how to proceed from here? (how of execution)

MANAGEMENT MASTER MIND

CHAPTER 18

NEEDS

'What a person needs is always more than
what they say! Always!'

EDWARD IRVING WORTIS

This section will use more examples applicable to engagement with external customers than with conversation partners. This may give the impression that understanding needs and the rest of the engagement excellence is more applicable to engagement outside of the organisation than internal engagement. That is, however, not true and it is a common mistake that internal departments believe that customer needs are only relevant for customer-facing departments. The reality is that customer-facing departments express their needs internally, based on engagement with external customers. It may, for example, be assumed that the request to reduce the turnaround time for an application processed by an internal department is based on customer needs and not made just because colleagues are impatient. Customer-facing departments have a duty to manage customer expectations by explaining what the requirements and process steps are, but that does not imply that internal departments do not also have to try to contribute to a better customer experience. Customer-facing departments act to a certain extent as messengers. They forward the customer's needs to the support departments, that should give clear feedback what can be expected by, and communicated to the customer. This only works if the support departments have an interest in and understanding of the customer's needs, and have the capability and attitude required to manage the customer's expectations. This is the reason why:

> *All departments are encouraged to use the same N(EX)3 approach, speak the same language and team up for the same customer who, in the end, pays the salaries for all.*

The examples in this chapter can therefore be used by both customer-facing departments in terms of what to do, but also by support departments in terms of how they could provide support.

PITFALLS TO AVOID: 'IT'S ABOUT US'

Most organisations claim to be customer-oriented, but often when the set-up of an organisation is analysed it becomes evident that the internal focus is much stronger than the external focus. Employees receive training on product knowledge, processes and procedures, and many other company-related issues, but hardly any training on professional customer engagement or needs analysis. Managers have both product and cost targets to meet, but they seldom have customer satisfaction targets or their own portfolio of customers. Only occasionally are employees sent on external customer service training sessions or is a customer survey conducted. This all shows that there is limited attention on the daily customer engagement.

These practices seem to indicate that customer satisfaction is being perceived more as a 'nice-to-have' than a core business 'need-to-have'. Organisations are generally not equipped to know, on a daily basis, what the expectations are for every single customer or whether their customers are satisfied with employee engagement.

> *There is a risk here that the customer will get the impression that the employees are more focused on satisfying the organisation's internal needs, rather than on finding the most suitable solution.*

Engagement excellence under the MILL model aims at respecting internal procedures and requirements, but not to the extent that the organisation gives customers the impression that 'it's about us'.

The first step towards achieving engagement excellence is, therefore, about understanding the customer's needs.

UNDERSTANDING NEEDS

> *It may not be clear from the beginning, but what the customer needs is not always the same thing as what they are asking for.*

It is very important to first find out what the customer is trying to achieve. For example, when a customer visits a bank and asks to open a new savings account, it may be assumed that the customer is only interested in saving money. However, the real need may not be simply to 'save'. The customer may intend to purchase something, and would like to have a buffer or back-up plan with money being set aside for unforeseen expenses or for generating income for the future. It is important to establish what the real need of the customer is, because the bank may have different options that will serve the customer better. These options could be insurances, investments for retirement or even personal loans.

It is also important to focus on the customer's needs for every new engagement with every new customer.

One customer may buy the most expensive, high-quality underwear but not bother spending a lot on a coat. Other customers may go for the cheapest underwear while driving a very expensive car. Only by asking the customers for their preference will it become clear what matters most to them. The new science of behavioural economics is trying to specify this irrational behaviour and marketing departments are trying to come up with new classifications of customer segments or 'avatars' as indicators for typical customer behaviour. However, there is no such classification and therefore it is best to find out by just asking the customer.

It is recommended that employees remain rigid in applying the four steps of the engagement excellence process. They must focus on identifying and understanding what the needs of the customer are at the beginning of every new engagement. When employees do not consistently follow up on the customer's needs during engagement, they may begin to assume that they already know the customer's preferences. This is despite the customer's preferences not having the same logic for every product in every situation.

> By failing to ask the right questions at the right time, and therefore failing to understand the customer's needs, poor recommendations will be made and the overall experience will be qualified as poor engagement.

The following four questions will help to understand a customer's needs:

- **What are you looking for? (Quality/quantity)**
  Asking this question provides an opportunity for the customer to explain what their expectations are. Some customers may explain the specifics of their expectations in technical details, while others may only

be interested in what the product will be able to do for them. This focus indicates what is the most relevant for the customer. It also helps to prepare the employee for the next steps of engagement excellence. Employees should be able to understand how the customer intends to use the products and services. This question can provide useful information about how frequently the product will be used, and indicate the performance or output quantity that the customer expects or needs. Details are crucial during this stage, but the kind of in-depth questions that need to be asked depend on the type of operation.

- **Why is this important to you? (Benefit/risk/dreams/fears)**
  This second question aims to clarify how the customer expects to benefit when using the product or service. This may sound obvious, but different customers might use the same product for different purposes. By better understanding what is important about the products or services, and why, employees are able to deliver an even better engagement. The answers should provide a detailed overview of expectations in terms of the benefits of the products and services delivered, and should even determine which risks and fears, if there are any, can be mitigated or reduced. This second question is both about the gains and the pains.

- **What are execution expectations? (Time/packaging/communication)**
  So far, the questions to identify needs have focused on the product and the customer but, in a highly competitive environment, it is also important to understand what customers expect from the customer-facing department as well as from the rest of the organisation. This third question is about finding out what kind of interaction the customer is looking for during the process and where value can be added in terms of the product and service delivered. This question can also be used to

identify areas where expectations could be exceeded. What needs to be done to meet the customer's expectations in terms of the processes before and after any engagement up to the moment of delivery? (Expectations should always be managed against expected timelines, how delivery can be performed to the highest standards in terms of packaging, as well as communication in terms of providing status updates and escalating when delayed, etc.).

- **Any other concern or dependency? (Objections/reservations)**
  The final question on needs is aimed at ring-fencing all possible outcomes and identifying what the conditions for the customer are in terms of budget, timeline and approval criteria. It could be that a third party, such as a spouse or manager, has to approve or can even veto the decision, and therefore their needs must also be accommodated. There could be a limited budget or a preference for a smaller pilot project to move faster. This specific question on concern or dependency is to obtain relevant information about whether the customer is able and willing to proceed if the needs, discussed during the first three questions, have already been met.

UNDERSTANDING INTERNAL NEEDS

Should the need for internal support arise from this external engagement, the same types of questions can be applied when engaging with conversation partners to understand their needs. For example, if front office employees require a proposal from the technical support department for a particular customer, the support department could ask their colleagues the following questions:

- 'What technical proposal are you looking for; what specs or features should be included?'
- 'What is it about the proposal that's important to the external customer and how or where will the solution be used?'
- 'When do you need the proposal and how would you like to be kept in the loop?'
- 'Is there anything else relevant for decision making/what are remaining dependencies to be aware of?'

The same principles and questions that have been used for external engagement should also be applied by internal departments when engaging with colleagues to create consistency and alignment.

> **A good understanding of the needs and expectations of the customer or conversation partner is important during any engagement.**

Customers want to be heard and are generally more than willing to provide detailed explanations when sincere interest is shown. Information received in this way is more useful and informative than that produced by market surveys. Trends in customer response can also be used as valuable input for marketing and product development departments.

The key skill to learn is how to ask open questions and allow the customer to speak freely without any interruptions. Customers should be encouraged to provide as much explanation as they can, for as long as they are willing to. The employee should also take clear notes to show that they are 'engaged' and genuinely interested in what the customer is saying. These notes are essential as they will be used as a checklist for each of the remaining steps in the engagement excellence process.

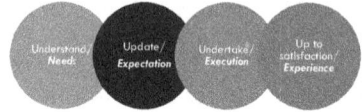

EXPECTATIONS → UPDATE

It is crucial to manage expectations. More appreciation can be expected if the customer understands requirements and processes, and especially how these are in their interests. This stage can also be used to create room to exceed expectations. If it is likely that expectations may not be met, so returning to the first step (understand) will allow for timely corrections.

Deliverable

- Explain what you expect to be able to deliver, based on your understanding

Process

- Explain the process of what the following (relevant) steps are, up to delivery

Cost, timing, dependencies

- Explain what the cost and timelines are, but also what could influence these

Engagement

- Explain what communication and engagement look like

CHAPTER 19:

EXPECTATIONS

'Exceed expectations, including your own.'

UNKNOWN

The second step in engagement excellence is about managing **expectations**. While the first step covered in the preceding chapter is about questioning the customer's needs, this second step requires the employee to provide feedback about processes, requirements, timescales and other matters that relate to their expectations. There are two goals here:

1. To verify whether the employee has a clear understanding of the customer's needs.

2. To determine ways to provide a service and outcome that exceeds the customer's expectations.

It is important for employees to discuss, with the customer, their own understanding of what the customer's needs are. To ensure their understanding is correct, they should provide a summary of it and then explain what the next steps will be. The employee should then verify that any work that will be done is in line with the customer's expectations. Where a customer indicates that they have not been well understood and their needs are likely not to be met, the employee must go back to the first step of engagement excellence and perhaps ask additional questions in order to establish a better understanding of the customer's needs.

It is important to note that this process creates transparency between both parties and ensures the entire experience stands out from competitors.

> *When employees and customers mutually understand what the expectations and needs are, engagements will automatically be more productive and therefore working relationships strengthened. Conducting this tailor-made approach of treating all customers as unique individuals and managing their expectations is crucial to stay ahead of competition.*

When the products or solutions are identical, customers will be more likely to take their business to an organisation that follows this process.

PITFALLS TO AVOID: 'WE THINK IT'S OBVIOUS'

> *Where organisations fail to make serious efforts to engage with customers and manage their expectations, they are perceived to be bureaucratic and internally focused.*

An example is when a customer is asked to complete various forms but is not told why they must do this, what the forms are for or what will happen once they are completed. Another example is when front office employees leave a customer waiting for long periods before returning. They provide no explanation to the customer of where they are going, how long they will be gone or even what they are doing. In both examples, the organisation believes that what they're doing and why they're doing it 'is obvious', but the customer is left wondering what is happening and where they even come into the picture.

Customers are not always made aware of the internal processes that oganisations have implemented to guarantee quality or to comply with internal or external regulations, and they are probably also not interested in knowing all the details behind what is happening on the processing side. However, it should be explained that these processes add value for them, the customer, even when they involve a waiting period or require the customer to supply additional information. When customers are not kept informed about what is happening with their request or what the relevance and added value of the shared information is, the organisation's internal processes will have a negative impact on customer satisfaction levels.

MANAGING EXPECTATIONS.

For expectations to be managed properly, employees should have a clear understanding of why the procedures or dependencies that a customer may perceive as cumbersome are in those same customer's interests.

For example, when a flight has been delayed due to the late arrival of another plane, an announcement is usually made. This announcement is much more acceptable when customers are informed that under no circumstances will quality control be affected or will safety checks be rushed to maintain the flight schedule. Customers can appreciate and respect that the new departure time is uncertain as long as a commitment is made to provide regular status updates. The most frustrating thing for any passenger would be radio silence – not receiving any communication about when the next flight will be, what the problem is or what will happen next.

Exceeding expectations can be achieved by proper managing of expectations. Consider the following scenarios:

- When passengers are told that their flight will take eight hours to reach its destination, but it arrives an hour late without them being informed, they will be very frustrated.

- When passengers are told that their flight will take ten hours, but the pilot announces at the half-way point that he will try his best to go faster and the plane lands after nine hours, they will be very happy and grateful.

Interestingly, both flights take nine hours.

> **The difference between happiness and frustration is therefore managing customer expectations – lowering expectations creates room to produce higher satisfaction levels.**

Employees should be encouraged to think more proactively about how customer expectations can be exceeded:

- How can small extras be provided in order to surprise customers?
- What can be done to make a service more convenient?
- How can time be saved?
- What new features can be added to a product and so on?

When managing expectations, the following four topics need to be addressed in order for the customer to believe that the employee has clearly understood and accurately captured their needs. This also provides more opportunities for the employees to exceed expectations.

- **The product/service**
  As soon as a customer believes the employee has neither paid attention to them nor understood their requirements, they will no longer listen

to what the employee says. For this reason, the employee should always begin by confirming their understanding of the customer's expectations by rephrasing what the customer said. Where it is clear that a customer is likely to investigate their options with competitors, it is worth including an additional feature that the customer has not asked about – one that is either unique or directly related to their needs. This is to show them that you are willing to do more than what was originally expected.

- **The company/department**

  The next step is to make it very clear what added value the company and/or department will bring to what has been discussed. Proof should also be provided to substantiate those claims or offers, such as the company's years of experience or large customer base and so on. It could also make sense to explain that the organisation guarantees to provide the quality levels promised through guarantees, quality control, good service and so forth. Customers are happy to listen to information about the professionalism of the organisation and the guaranteed quality levels, provided that the benefits are explained – that is, ISO certification, return policies or other quality assurances.

- **The process**

  The customer is generally not interested in the internal operations of an organisation, except where there are dependencies and processes that can influence their overall experience and, therefore, their level of satisfaction. It is important to inform the customer, upfront, about what will happen next – from the moment the conversation ends until the next arranged conversation or meeting, or even when the customer begins to make use of the product/service. Where there is a risk that the customer may perceive anything about the processes as bureaucratic, cumbersome or slow, the employee must be able to provide clear explanations for why these process steps have been put in place – that is, they are there to ensure quality control reliability and so forth. It is important to make sure, when employees deal with customers, that they fully understand their own organisation so they can explain the added value of internal processes.

- **Your role**
  It will be helpful to advise the customer what further support they can expect to receive, and also what will happen if the employee they are dealing with is not around or cannot be reached. An explanation about the engagement excellence process should be provided to give the customer an insight into why a certain approach has been taken, and what the next steps are expected to be. The final step of the engagement excellence process (explained later in this chapter), aims at getting useful input from customers about any areas that need to be improved. But, in order to do so at a later stage, the customer should be made aware, upfront, about the employee's eagerness to create the very best experience by using the engagement excellence approach.

MANAGING INTERNAL EXPECTATIONS

The process of managing expectations also applies to organisations that have internal requests for support.

Imagine the IT department has to develop a report for the manager of another department. The same verification process needs to be followed to establish whether needs have been understood. This should be done by providing a summary and an explanation of what will happen next and how much time it will take to fulfil the request, and by asking what kind of information is required and for what purpose. Departments that aim to exceed the expectations of their colleagues can be very stimulating for team spirit. For example, a product department asked to come up with a proposal might include some extra features without additional costs, and an IT department might go the extra mile when asked to supply specific data by also providing a helpful graphic presentation.

It is evident that managing expectations is a very powerful tool to use in the engagement process, both within and outside the organisation. It provides opportunities for corrections at an early stage and for improvements to be considered as soon as it becomes clear that needs may not have been understood. At the same time, it is during this phase of the engagement process that the employee is able to develop new ideas about how expectations can be exceeded.

> *During any of the four steps of managing expectations, not only is the customer given an opportunity to respond, but the employee also has time to consider how expectations can be exceeded.*

Employees should be able to provide a clear, precise summary of the customer's needs to confirm that they have understood them. They must also provide a clear explanation of procedures and processes, or the next steps to be taken, without using technical jargon or irrelevant details. They should be able to develop their own creative ideas on how to exceed expectations. If this step, which is intended to help manage expectations, is managed well, then all the required input will be available for the next step of the engagement excellence process, which is about its execution.

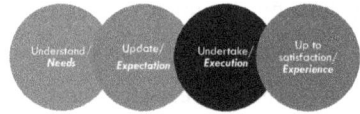

EXECUTION → UNDERTAKE

In the update phase we 'say what we do', so it is important in this phase to 'do what we say'. The execution process should have some checklists to ensure that customer expectations are met. Overall production processes cannot be tailored to individual needs, but small personal adjustments can make a big difference. Support departments will perform best if they can also identify with customers.

The execution checklist could contain expectations around:

Expected usage/benefits

Progress communication

Specific wishes (features)

Most relevant differentiator

MANAGEMENT
MASTER MIND

CHAPTER 20:

EXECUTION

*'There is only one boss. The customer. And he can fire
everybody in the company from the chairman on down, simply
by spending his money elsewhere.'*

SAM WALTON

The previous chapter focused on determining whether customer needs have been well understood, then managing expectations by explaining what will be done. In other words, the communication will have a large component that will 'say what we do'. The next step of engagement excellence is about execution or, in other words, 'do what we say'. There should, of course, be alignment between 'say what we do' and 'do what we say'.

> **Where commitments were made during the managing expectations phase, these should be met during the execution phase.**

If these commitments cannot be met, there is an obligation to provide the customer with an explanation of why the commitment cannot be met, and at that moment discuss possible solutions or options for a new commitment. This will allow continued management of the customer's expectations.

In order to align efforts in the customer's interest, clear communication and a mutual understanding are required between both the departments that interact directly with customers and the production/support departments.

It is important that support departments also understand what expectations the customer has shared, what is therefore required, and what was committed to be done.

> **When departments work together as a team, both sides must respect each other's responsibilities and limitations.**

For example, the sales department cannot make all kinds of promises to customers that require the production/support department to do the impossible. On the other hand, the production/support department should avoid having too many restrictive rules and requirements that are only protecting their internal interests. It is recommended for respective teams to have joint action improvement meetings to see what can be done to strengthen cooperation and teamwork.

PITFALLS TO AVOID – 'WE TRY OUR BEST'

Based on their own internal assessment, most departments believe they are performing well when it comes to executing a job. For example, production/support departments may use their own benchmark to measure quality and speed of output. Under this self-assessment, the quality and timing may seem perfectly reasonable and acceptable:

> **Pitfalls occur when the needs of external customers cannot be accommodated under the internally focused standard approach.**

In other words, when there is no flexibility to accommodate the specific needs or requirements of individual customers. Managers may rationalise this lack of flexibility by explaining that processes cannot be disturbed for individual cases, as that would decrease efficiency or could increase costs, but in order to meet the customer's needs, some flexibility could make a big difference.

Customer-facing departments also require timely communication about changes within the production/ support department that may result in delays. This type of internal engagement about communicating progress or escalating issues when there are delays is generally not considered to be part of production/support departments' core duties. Such departments may try to resolve issues themselves, but fail to communicate potential delays that could have an impact on customer satisfaction. Internal departments should not claim 'we try our best', as some flexibility and proper communication is also required from them in order to stay aligned with departments that face customers directly. In this way, production departments indirectly also take responsibility for satisfying the needs of the external customer.

FLEXIBILITY FOR EXECUTION

A true customer service-oriented company will not only focus on standardising the processes for efficiency and quality control, but will also allow for some flexibility in their processes.

Car manufacturers understand that the many customers they have want to be treated as individuals by being given a choice of colour, fabric type, rim design and so forth. Manufacturers are able to build these preferences into their production processes. This kind of flexibility does not always require end-to-end process re-engineering, but flexibility could also be achieved by allowing for manageable exceptions in existing processes. The intention is to satisfy the external customer needs without having a significant and negative impact on efficiency levels.

Embedding flexibility requires some give-and-take from all stakeholders, but the benefits of increased customer satisfaction are clearly worth the effort.

> *Maintaining the balance between flexibility and efficiency is more sustainable in the long run than when the focus is on efficiency alone.*

One successful Spanish clothing company, the Zara group, already understood that through making improvements to its planning and by re-allocating production back to Spain, they became more flexible. This flexibility has allowed Zara to have up to twenty new collections per year instead of the traditional four.

Understanding what the dependencies are that make processes inflexible opens up many opportunities to work towards becoming more customer-focused.

ACTION IMPROVEMENTS FOR EXECUTION

Below are some areas that could be considered for finding better alignment or more flexibility during execution.

- **Clarity**

  Involving production/support departments when customer-facing departments have their internal discussion on the needs of the customers can help to get more clarity among the departments. By having a better understanding of what the customer expects to achieve, the support department may be able to come up with a better overall proposition or some useful suggestions about what can be done differently in order to exceed customer expectations.

- **Capacity**

  There should be transparency between the two partnering departments about availability and production capacity. Any capacity constraints must be made known so that departments working together are able to identify where the bottlenecks will be, and how any issues that may arise as a result will be addressed. It is important to know the available production capacity to be able to inform and manage the expectations of the (external) customer. The departments must also be able to adequately track progress and manage customer expectations in terms of any commitments made.

- **Preparation**

  It shouldn't be taken for granted that achievements happen spontaneously. In order to achieve something, proper preparation is key. From the beginning, there needs to be a clear understanding about: a) what needs to be achieved; b) what planning must be put in place in terms of when and how things must be done; c) what could potentially cause a delay, and d) what analyses can be performed so that measures can be put in place to avoid delays. Knowing and respecting each other's challenges could help to improve teamwork significantly. It should be communicated at the start that unforeseen 'urgencies' may occur on a daily basis, and these must take priority. Once this fact is known, time can be allocated during the planning stage to deal with challenges, despite not yet knowing what they are.

- **Focus**

  As specified above, internal support/production departments may be more focused on efficiency and cost than on speed or external customers. It is a balancing act where guidance is required by senior management to assist employees in setting priorities. It should, however, be made clear that the highest priority, in any department, should be to focus on customer needs.

  > *It is unrealistic to expect customer-facing departments to deliver excellent customer satisfaction when internal departments focus on efficiency only, and not on the customer.*

  Joint action improvement meetings can change the focus of how projects are executed internally by balancing the interest of both departments and creating mutual understanding and agreement on actions that will increase teamwork.

INTERNAL EXECUTION

Larger organisations may find it more challenging to engage all employees in the contribution towards an overall result. Employees working in support/production departments may not realise that the work they carry out contributes to both customer satisfaction and the overall performance of the organisation. This implies that:

> *The need for alignment and flexibility between internal departments can be achieved by creating mutual understanding of how each department operates.*

The same recommendation of having regular joint action improvement meetings applies, which allows departments to team up to determine what can be done more often and also what can be done better.

Where there is no room for flexibility and/or where there is a limited understanding between departments that are supposed to cooperate with each other, the goal of achieving engagement excellence can be easily ruined during the execution phase. However, when departments avoid working in isolation (silos) and show interest in each other's challenges and needs, this will have a positive impact on the overall engagement excellence.

Engagement
excellence

Understand/
Needs — Update/
Expectation — Undertake/
Execution — Up to
satisfaction/
Experience

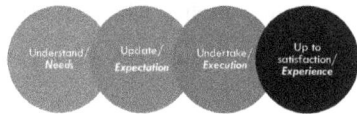

EXPERIENCE → SATISFACTION

This last phase is meant to get feedback from the customer as input for learning and improvement. Understanding what went well is important, but the real lessons learned should come from suggestions and critiques. Showing eagerness to receive input on areas for improvement is essential to improve the relationship, but also for more generic development to become a master in engagement excellence.

The following questions can be asked to check overall satisfaction:

Where could we do better in the end product?

Where could we have done better in the process?

What area is less than or similar to our competitors and how do we compare?

What follow-up could we do in the future to check whether you are still happy?

The ForYou/4U approach also allows direct feedback from the customers on the four steps of engagement excellence.

MANAGEMENT
MASTER MIND

CHAPTER 21:

EXPERIENCE

'Your most unhappy customers are your greatest
source of learning.'

BILL GATES

This final step of engagement excellence is about the importance of gathering feedback from the customer or conversation partner in order to review their overall **experience**.

> **Any feedback received about overall performance should be used as a teaching or learning tool.**

Customer feedback on their experience, can also be beneficial for the action improvement debriefing meetings held at the end of the week. It shouldn't be taken for granted that feedback on experiences will be provided, so there is always a need to explicitly ask for feedback. Once feedback is received, it becomes mandatory to use it for further action improvements as part of continuous learning.

Performance analysis will be done by reviewing data generated but, generally, information derived from statistical data also has its limitations in terms of added value. Statistical data can indicate where the problems or opportunities are, but not always *what* the challenges or opportunities are:

> **Experience in the MILL model is more related to customer perception than to factual data, as only the customer can determine whether expectations have been exceeded.**

The best improvements can be made by asking the customers themselves questions about what can be done better, more or even differently, in future engagements.

PITFALLS TO AVOID: WE SUPPOSE 'THIS IS IT'

At the time of delivery, many organisations focus more on their products than on the quality of engagement with the customer. It is often assumed the customer will be satisfied once the product/solution is delivered. This final step, however, is the moment the customer has been waiting for. It is the stage when decisions will be made about whether any future engagements will take place and whether the organisation will get a 'like' on Facebook or other endorsements.

Despite the importance of this final engagement step, organisations often show a lack of sincere interest in the customer's overall perceptions by failing to ask specific questions about their experience. For example, when a waiter in a restaurant asks you whether you enjoyed the meal and you provide a detailed explanation about why you did not enjoy it, the waiter may offer you a free cup of coffee as compensation. However, this kind of compensation may not necessarily make you want to return to that same restaurant. This is because the root causes of the problem were not properly assessed, nor were explanations provided, and it is not clear to the customer what would be different the next time they dine at that restaurant.

SATISFACTION SURVEYS

Organisations generally don't incorporate a proper evaluation process that can be completed by staff members in the final stage of liaising with their customers. Instead, they tend to outsource their surveys to companies that gather customer feedback in ways such as checking the net promoter score (for example, by asking 'Would you promote this organisation to your friends?'). These types of surveys only aim to achieve an understanding of trends for statistical benchmarking. They are generally not used for immediate learning and improvement as the quality of the data does not create an in-depth understanding of how to improve the overall experience. The overwhelming increase in these kinds of non-personal surveys, as well as the lack of follow-up, will make customers less likely to take part in them. This will have an impact on the quality of data and, therefore, the value they provide, and the customer will feel even more reluctant to cooperate.

The feedback collated by external surveys is considered to be more objective, but this assumes that the customer may not be able to provide honest feedback directly to the employee, and that the employee may try to manipulate the response from the customer. There may be situations when third parties could be used to collect internal feedback in order to overcome these challenges. However:

> The quality and usability of direct feedback not only generates a more direct way of learning, but also creates the opportunity for immediate correction and improvement.

The employee is empowered to correct mistakes and does not have to wait for the marketing department to produce a statistical report that hardly gives insights into what can be improved. This is why the checking, by *employees*, of customers' perceived experience has been incorporated in engagement excellence under the MILL model.

Even if an employee tries their best to avoid any of the above pitfalls, it is ultimately still the customer who is the best judge of whether their expectations were met. If the employee shows a sincere interest in establishing where and how improvements can be made in the entire engagement process, any feedback can be used to iron out flaws perceived by the customer. If this final step in the engagement excellence process is performed well, the customer will become an ambassador for not only the product, but also the entire organisation. This is the best kind of marketing an organisation can have.

THE FORYOU-4U APPROACH

There is an approach that can be used when assessing customer experience called the 'ForYou-4U' approach. These four 'U's stand for the activities in any engagement: Understand, Update, Undertake and Up to Satisfaction, which are in fact actions related to the N(EX)3 model. When using this approach, it should be made clear to the customer that any feedback they provide will be used to make improvements as part of the organisation's willingness to offer them engagement excellence. :

> *Customers need to be made aware, from the beginning, that there is no such thing as negative feedback, as all feedback can be used to improve the engagement.*

The customer's perceptions are their realities and they should be encouraged to be truthful when giving their feedback.

The 4U approach is undertaken by asking the customer the following questions:

- **4U dimension: Understand (Needs)**
  How would you rate our efforts in trying to understand what your needs were and how these could be best served? In other words, do you believe the employee understood you well enough to determine how value could be added?
  This questions the customer's needs, expected timelines and what they believe to be important.

- **4U dimension: Update (Expectations)**
  How would you rate the feedback you received detailing our understanding of what your expectations are and how we explained what would be done to meet you needs?
  This questions whether the customer was provided with sufficient information about what the end results would look like, how long the process would take and what it would entail. Was it made clear from the beginning what the customer should expect in terms of what would be done and by whom? Was it explained why the customer needed to complete forms and why the relevant information was required?

- **4U dimension: Undertake (Execution)**
  How would you rate the final result – were requests executed effectively and were expectations met?
  This questions whether the organisation delivered what the customer needed, and whether the process was effective and without surprises.

How was the quality of communication about progress made and possible delays to meet the customer's expectations? Did the customer feel there was enough flexibility in accommodating their needs during production/execution of the job?

- **4U dimension: Up to Satisfaction (Experience)**
  How would you rate your overall experience from beginning to end, also considering the area's for improvement?
  This questions the customer's overall perception of the organisation and helps to identify ways to improve. This covers all details from the time the customer enters the organisation up to delivery phase. It asks the customer what they did or did not like, and what they did not understand. These are areas where the customer may believe competitors are better, and also where they believe the organisation could differentiate themselves from their competitors.

Each of the four questions should have two follow-up questions:

1. Do you have any examples or explanations about why certain scores were given?
2. Do you have any suggestions about how scores could be improved?

The customers must be encouraged to provide as much detail as they like about their concerns or suggestions. An appropriate question to ask the customer, as a way of encouraging them to provide more feedback, is 'What else?'

Asking these questions is not the end of the engagement process. The customer may still want to be advised about what the organisation will do with their feedback. They may also want to know how, when and in what way action improvements will be embedded in the future. If that commitment can only be shared after the next action improvement meeting, then the customer should be called the following week and given feedback. High ratings given by the customer may also need to be followed up by the manager to confirm the reliability of the feedback, and also to thank the customer for their compliments. This kind of follow-up is considered to be time well spent, as the customer will inevitably discuss their positive experience with others who may, as a result, become customers in the future.

Net promoter score versus ForYou/4U

Comparing NPS with ForYou/4U	Using NPS		Using ForYou/4U
Simplicity of engagement	Very simple and quick	◄►	Less simple and longer
Root cause satisfaction specified	Not clear	◄►	Clear which category
Allows for clarification score	Not included	◄►	Part of the process
Usage for development	More statistical and control	◄►	Part of engagement; input for development
Can be used best for	Annual general image assessment	◄►	Quarterly customer portfolio assessment per employee

INTERNAL EXPERIENCE FEEDBACK

Asking for feedback on the overall experience should also be a standard procedure for internal support/production departments to help them understand where they can improve. Colleagues may be less confrontational when providing feedback because they don't want to damage team spirit, but even if a rating is 9/10, there is room for improvement. Questions can still be asked about what can be done differently to achieve a perfect 10/10.

> *Feedback is important when growing and grooming employees as they climb the career ladder.*

It is therefore essential to provide constructive feedback in order for them to learn from their mistakes and successes. During internal engagements, feedback should be mutual and constructive, forward looking, to team up for improvement.

> *There are times when support/production departments may not have been sufficiently informed about expectations and may also receive impossible requests from other departments.*

To sort out these kinds of issues smoothly, internal discussions should be encouraged in order to find mutually acceptable solutions moving forward.

It will be unfortunate if opportunities are missed when reviewing customers' overall experiences simply because proper closing engagements are not conducted. These engagements allow their expectations and perceptions to be managed. These perceptions determine the organisation's overall image, and it should be highlighted that poor impressions spread faster than good ones. Any potential negative cycles can be managed and turned into positive ones by showing a willingness to learn from the customers' perceptions, and by applying the lessons learned during future engagements – either with the same customers or with other customers.

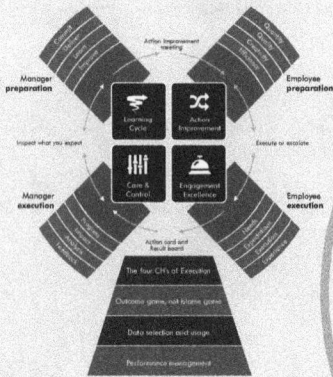

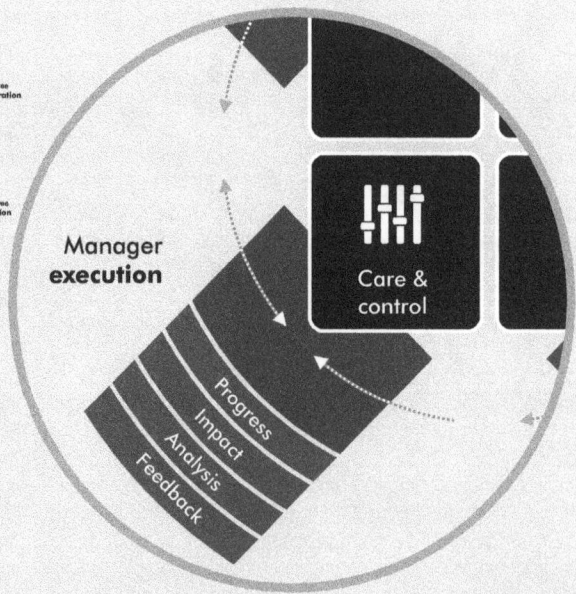

Manager
execution

Care &
control

Progress
Impact
Analysis
Feedback

PART 6:
CARE AND
CONTROL

The final blade of the MILL model is **care** and **control**. It is essential for a manager to show care and control towards employees to keep the process of action improvement moving. The kind of intervention required under care and control depends on the progress made and results achieved by the individual employee.

There should never be a situation in which a manager shows no interest at all in their employees.

Every employee deserves attention, and when they receive it on a regular basis the result will be consistent improvement in their results.

It is recommended that a manager schedules at least 30–45 minutes per day to focus on this kind of employee engagement. It is unlikely that a manager will ever find the time to progress any engagement without this initial proper planning. If the manager is not consistent about these kinds of follow-ups and believes there are valid reasons why engagements should only take place occasionally, employees may begin to take assignments given to them by the manager less seriously. Employees may think, 'If you do not care, I do not care, so if you do not inspect what you expect, it is clear that other topics are more important for you.'

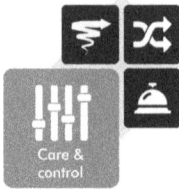

PROGRESS

There is always a reason to postpone new behaviour. And the longer the wait, the less likely it is that the new behaviour will happen. A manager cannot 'assume' and has a duty to show interest. A manager too busy to manage their employees is like a fisherman too busy to fish. In the end, all staff results contribute to the manager's result, therefore it is in the manager's interest to manage progress.

It is crucial to check progress within thirty-six hours of creating commitment to find out and address the following situations:

Not even started

Half-heartedly started

Seriously started, but no or little impact

Up and running

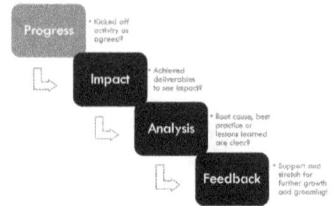

MANAGEMENT
MASTER MIND

CHAPTER 22

PROGRESS

'The secret of getting ahead is getting started.'

BILL GATES

The first building block of the care and control blade is **progress**. It is recommended to start having engagements on progress made within thirty-six hours of employees making their action improvement commitments. Any postponement by the manager to show care could be perceived as insufficient support for the employee in their endeavour to stretch further. When the manager does the first follow-up after the action improvement meeting, there are four possible scenarios that the manager may need to address.

NOT EVEN STARTED

Under the execute or escalate rule, it is unacceptable for employees to not escalate any of their concerns or possible delays. The commitment made by the employee during the action improvement meeting is to begin activities the same day or at least within twenty-four hours. Employees are expected to have their action card developed after the AIM so that not only results commitments are clear, but also action commitments.

> *Not executing commitment, but also not escalating it,*
> *is considered to be a 'breach'.*

The 'three strikes and you're out' rule will be applied here. This means that every breach will be counted as a strike, and after three strikes the staff member will receive either a verbal or written warning. The manager has to apply this rule consistently after clearly announcing the principles and processes. When breaches are not acted upon, this will undermine the rule of executing or escalating and will have a negative impact on both the execution of commitments and their results.

When a breach occurs, the manager first explains the principles and consequences of a breach and then establishes what is required in order to get back on track. This sequence is important, because employees may find an opportunity to make excuses or talk their way out of trouble by blaming somebody else for their mistakes. The root cause of the problem can never be shifted to somebody else as there is never an excuse not to escalate, and in such cases the manager should challenge the employee to explain what will be done differently the next time. This allows the employee to show an eagerness for improvement and take ownership of the situation to avoid it being repeated.

STARTED IN A HALF-HEARTED WAY

The second situation that could occur when the manager is exercising care and control by doing follow-up on employee commitments is finding evidence of poor progress. In this case there is little or perhaps even nothing to show that could support the employee's claims that proper effort has been put into performing the agreed tasks. Employees may come up with stories or excuses to explain why they failed to meet their agreed commitments or did not even prepare their action card.

It is useful to ask a few questions about where things might have gone wrong, such as:

- 'Was it made clear enough at the beginning what needed to be done?'
- 'Is the employee capable of doing what was agreed upon?'
- 'Was sufficient preparation put in place?'
- 'Could the failure be simply due to the employee having a negative attitude?'

When employees respond to the manager, they need to specify exactly where and what changes will be made so that the manager can check these during the next engagement. In line with the commitments made during the action improvement meeting in front of the whole team, feedback on poor work progress can also be made public as long as it is done with respect to the competencies and circumstances of the individual – hard on tasks, soft on people.

Managers who fail to address under-performers will fail to take advantage of the power that peer pressure has among colleagues. When the group has made commitments to certain goals, the manager should continue endorsing these group goals for each individual.

When the manager accepts under-performance for one employee, this lowers the standards for other employees and could even decrease their motivation.

Employees do not like to be stretched when the manager is simultaneously seen to be accepting another colleague's lack of performance.

ACTIONS COMMITTED AS AGREED, BUT POOR RESULTS

This is a situation in which actions were carried out by the employees according to their commitments as captured on their action card, but the results are not (yet) as expected. The manager can ask challenging questions to stimulate the employee to look for the root causes for results below expectation, but the tone of voice should be positive. Under the MILL model, lessons learned can be as valuable as results, as long as these lessons are being used for new action improvements.

When following up with an employee, it can make sense to ask the employee to review what transpired to identify what could have influenced the outcome of the engagement. This could be how they prepared for the engagement, what structure and language was used during the engagement, or even the setting of the meeting. The following questions can be useful:

- How did the employee structure the engagement in terms of steps taken?

- What were the triggers to change direction or go to the next phase?

- What efforts were taken to get to know the customer's personal circumstances and what their expectations were?

The goal is to come up with ideas about what should be considered for action improvement for future engagements.

The employee should respond to the manager's questions by explaining:

- **S** → What the situation was
- **B** → The relevant behaviours
- **O** → The outcome
- **L** → What was learned and therefore will be applied in the next attempt.

The manager should commend the employee for their efforts, offer to provide support and encourage them to keep coming up with ideas for adjustments in their action improvements.

EMPLOYEE IS SUCCESSFUL IN ACTIONS AND RESULTS

When following up, the manager may also come across situations where employees have not only met their action commitments, but their results have also met or exceeded expectations. The employee, of course, deserves to be complimented, but still needs to be followed up in case there are recommendations and checks to be done. The manager could, for example, check whether these well-performing employees were able to combine the good results achieved with their normal daily work routine and their usual teamwork. There is a risk that individuals who are too eager to out-perform will not be able to execute their other tasks or, if they do, they will put little effort into them and the quality of the routine work will be low.

The goal is always to achieve sustainable growth, which means balancing new assignments with existing duties.

The manager should also find out whether these well-performing employees understand exactly what, in detail, contributed most to their successful result. They should know how to replicate their success, and therefore be able to provide their colleagues with valuable insights. Where they can identify what their best practices are, these can be shared verbally at the end-of-week debrief and celebrated with the whole team. Colleagues should be encouraged to apply the same practices in their action plan for the following week.

The final question the manager has to ask when engaging with these well-performing employees is whether there is still room for further action improvement. These high-performing employees are in the lead so far, but as the rest of the team is also developing, they cannot ignore opportunities for growth and personal development if they want to stay in the lead. High performers may get bored or feel that they are no longer growing, so they should also show that they can be in the lead when it comes to the action improvements.

Regardless of whether an employee is performing well, failing badly or is performing somewhere between these two extremes, it is vital for a manager to show care and control by following up in a timely fashion on progress made. Depending on the progress made, the different types of responses described above should be utilised.

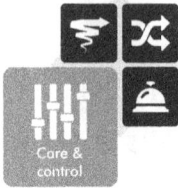

Progress · Kicked off activity as agreed?

Impact · Achieved deliverables to see impact?

Analysis · Root cause, best practice or lessons learned are clear?

Feedback · Support and stretch for further growth and grooming!

Care & control

IMPACT

Part of learning is understanding the message that can be derived from the performance data. A multi-dimensional view will automatically result in a better view. The added value of every approach is different, but by combining the views it will become clear where to dig deeper for root causes.

If some progress is made evaluation can start by comparing effort with outcome, and also use other means of comparison:

Results vs plan ➜ budget + assumptions

Results vs time ➜ trend + market

Result vs peers ➜ benchmark + best practice

Effort vs impact ➜ efficiency + leading indicators

MANAGEMENT
MASTER MIND

CHAPTER 23

IMPACT

'You always learn a lot more when you lose

than when you win.'

AFRICAN PROVERB

Both the manager and employees will monitor the impact of action im-provements by comparing the actions that were committed after the action improvement meeting with the results that were achieved. The action card and result board are used for the weekly tracking of actions and result goals in order to understand the correlation between the two.

> *Measuring impact is important for discovering how employees can work smarter by achieving more with less effort.*

For example, the employee with the highest impact (best results per action) can be used as a benchmark to compare the scores of other team members. This provides a starting point for discussions on what worked well and what did not work (see also next paragraph on benchmarking). Knowing what did not work well indicates where the organisation has opportunities to improve.

It is, however, also important to check whether the team and individual performances are in line with other performance indicators within the or-ganisation, such as budgets or market shares.

> *Examining and combining various sources of information can create additional clarity on root causes for problems in the organisation, and therefore where to look for performance improvement.*

Impact analysis for short-term improvement can be further developed and expanded into both predictive analysis (proactive) and scenario planning (reactive). Predictive analysis means that employees and management can predict the results when there is an increase in activity in a certain area. Scenario planning can be done by identifying external trends that already have an impact on the organisation's success, and therefore should be continuously monitored for timely action if significant change is likely to occur.

Monitoring and measuring impact is part of care and control. Staff should be involved in assessing information to enhance their understanding and, therefore, empower them to learn. This kind of impact analysis can be done during the daily progress engagement between the manager and the employee or during the weekly debrief with the whole team.

> *Staff should not only understand what needs to be done, but also why it has to be done.*

This can be achieved by the manager explaining the bigger picture. Involving staff in discovering the current position and getting buy-in for the new direction is very powerful for creating ownership. Those staff who learn quickly how to read data and translate these insights into action could be identified as management potential.

Below are four examples of what data to use, and how to use it, to better understand the impact of actions.

RESULTS VERSUS PLAN

Results versus plan refers to the basic analysis that most companies do. Whether it is an annual plan called a budget, or a quarterly plan, the principles are more or less similar – results are examined to see whether they have met or fallen below expectations. There are, however, some pitfalls in this kind of analysis that are not always considered.

For example, as there will always be uncertainties, most budgets or plans have to be based on assumptions. This can have a big impact on the results. If underlying assumptions are incorrect, an unrealistic budget may have been set and continuing with it will be very demotivating. If, however, assumptions were made about potential setbacks that did not occur and therefore the budget was too prudent, the budget would have to be corrected upwards. In this case, the results will come from conservative budgeting, not hard or smart work. Employees involved in the budget process should not only be stretched in setting targets, but also challenged on realistic assumptions.

Management can also make the mistake of only paying attention to the underperforming, or 'red', areas when comparing results with the plan. If results are 'green' (in line with plan), there is often no further questioning. However, it could be very interesting in these situations to find out what exactly went well. Areas of strength and opportunities should be assessed in order to explore even more of the great results for faster growth. Spending time on understanding exactly what was done by the employee to get something right shows appreciation and recognition for staff effort, which increases the motivation to continue and expand, as high performers want to share their success and be in the spotlight.

RESULTS VERSUS TIME

Results should also be analysed over a period of time. This could be done by measuring how the gap – or excess – between the plan and the results develop over time. If the gap gets narrower, despite current under-performance, this is a positive trend and should be appreciated. If the results so far have been ahead of the plan, but the amount of excess is shrinking, then warning signals should go out; in short, losses could be positive (if declining) and profits could be concerning (if declining). Ideally these kinds of comparisons should be shown in line graphs to create more visual clarity. Showing results vs. plan in trend lines and extrapolating these trends will make it clear whether lines are diverging or converging, and therefore make it possible to predict when the lines are expected to cross where a profit becomes a loss or the other way around.

Trend lines should also be used if there is a seasonal pattern. The effect of these patterns should be clearly specified in the monthly budget based on this knowledge. The seasonal pattern of the previous year(s) should be used in the same line-graph for the current year in order to identify new trends. Seasonality patterns can change, but there should still be an effort to understand them. Just assuming that 'this year the season seems to be starting late' is not an acceptable analysis. To filter out these kinds of 'stories' and uncertainties, trends can be best measured by including market or competitor data if available.

RESULT VERSUS PEERS

The quickest team analysis can be done by comparing employees with their peers. This can be done within a team by using the action card and result board, but it is also recommended to compare different teams that have similar assignments within an organisation.

> **Checking team performance rather than comparing individual performances is a very powerful tool for stimulating teamwork.**

Too much focus on individual performance could create less cooperation between employees, leading to a lack of synergies and exchange of best practices within the team, and therefore lower overall results.

Another advantage of comparing team performance is that most excuses given by under-performers can be countered. If a certain team is underperforming but is blaming the systems, the support or the products, then the manager can easily point to a different team that has to deal with exactly the same circumstances but is still able to perform. The best team performance will always become the benchmark, and be used to challenge other teams to aim for this proven, achievable level is likely to result in more high scores, or even higher scores that will again raise the bar for all teams.

RESULT VERSUS IMPACT

The last type of analysis, which requires the largest involvement from staff, is to define and measure so-called leading indicators. The analyses described above are related to lagging indicators, such as financial indicators, that show what happened in the past. Leading indicators, however, are provided by the predictive analysis described in the introduction of this section.

> **Leading indicators are indicators that can, to a certain extent, predict what financial outcome can be expected.**

What efforts are directly correlated to results and, therefore, qualify to become leading indicators

The intention here is to understand the correlation between effort and result or, in other words, the impact of the action. If, for example, quicker follow-up on sales quotes has shown to deliver better sales results (and the follow-up time can be measured), then the turnaround time between quotes and follow-up could become a leading impact indicator. Leading impact indicators can quantify the activity that differentiates something as best practice, and once this correlation has been discovered management and staff should start monitoring these indicators. Continuously and closely monitoring the actions of each step in the sales process (the sales funnel) will also create a better understanding what efforts are most effective (have the highest impact).

Measuring impact to see whether efforts are paying off and whether progress is in line with expectations can be done in multiple ways. Every approach will provide insights that can be used as input for another round of action improvement. Numbers are often tracked without properly discussing the information that can be derived from them.

> The MILL model encourages organisations to have a 'data-digestion' process to make sure that data analysis is always used to come up with action improvements.

Without this, data knowledge itself will never lead to better results.

Organisations may expect that more data will become available in the near future, which could make it even more complex to filter relevant information and use it to agree on action improvements. Alternating and combining the various sources of information for action improvement will show what data sources are most valuable for creating success. In order to get the best out of data and dig deeper into root causes, some additional analysis may be required and this is described in the next chapter.

ANALYSIS

Describing in words what the numbers show is not the same as analysis. Analysis is investigating what has influenced the numbers or, in other words, the root cause. Root causes beyond control should be considered as circumstances. Understanding root causes is especially important when performance expectations are not met.

The search for root causes can be guided by the following questions:

Where could the weakest link be?

How can this be monitored?

How could improvements be made?

When can this start?

CHAPTER 24:

ANALYSIS

'To repeat what other have said, requires education;
to challenge it requires brains.'

MARY POOLE

Checking progress is the first step of management's engagement with employees under care and control. This is done to find out whether they have started the actions they committed to. Checking impact is the second step. This is done to find out what the outcome has been so far and how this correlates to the various benchmarks and expectations, which helps to get an initial understanding of which steps in the process, or which actions, need further improvement. The third part of care and control is to **analyse**, with the staff involved, exactly *what* could be improved based on their initial experience executing the action commitments. This **analysis** step should be done to dig deeper for root causes in order to understand what have been the key contributors to success or failure so far, and which of those could be influenced by employees without additional support or resources.

This chapter will describe the following four categories of root causes that can be found with proper analysis:

1. It could be that only one (small) part of the execution has been weak, but is still having a big impact on the overall results. Identifying this **weakest link** and working out how to deal with it is the focus of this category of root cause.

2. If the strongest dependency cannot be managed, the root cause may seem to be beyond control. In this case the recommendation is to analyse what kind of **early warning** indicators can be monitored to circumvent or prepare for these external challenges.

3. If the root cause analysis shows that all new efforts have had limited impact so far, then the real problem was probably not solved, and the challenge is how to **stop the bleeding**.

4. The last root cause is related to poor attitude or limited excitement. This is where the concept of **quick wins** can be explored to get the team moving.

ANALYSIS FOR THE WEAKEST LINK

The strength of a chain is determined by the weakest link. This same principle applies to performance processes that can be broken down into smaller steps. The challenge, and therefore the opportunity, could be in:

- The capabilities (enough skills, competencies, resourcing?)
- The preparation (proper planning, enough tools?)
- The execution (needs clear, expectations managed?)
- The follow-up (timely action, overall experience?)

> *Understanding what the weakest link is will make clear what the likely root cause is for the low performance.*

This analysis can be done by breaking down the bigger process into smaller steps to see how every step was performed or could be improved. This kind of analysis can be done regardless of the overall performance, as there will always be a weakest link that provides an opportunity for improvement.

Even high performers are likely to have an area where they are less effective or less capable. For example, a very successful employee's weak link could be not being able to allocate more time to create even more results. The way to deal with this is understanding how to get rid of less relevant, time-consuming actions. The 'right people in the right place' also implies supporting employees in creating time to do what they are good at.

> **There is always an area that can be improved and small steps of continuous improvement will build champions.**

There is no added value for staff if the manager simply praises them and recommends that they 'continue to do what you are doing'. The duty of a manager is to groom employees and make people grow regardless of their performance level.

ANALYSIS FOR EARLY WARNING

In some cases, the analysis will show that the biggest dependency or the weakest link seems to be beyond control.

> **These root causes should be considered as circumstances, but that does not mean that they can be used as excuses for low performance going forward.**

There are two options for how to deal with these kinds of circumstances in a productive manner. The first option is to look for a workaround (alternative approach), and if a successful one is found this best practice should be kept on stand-by in case the same circumstances occur again. The second option is that the circumstances are such that further efforts really do not make sense, and therefore a different goal should be explored so as not to waste time.

For both options, it makes sense to have some monitoring that can identify early warning indicators that these circumstances are going to recur. For example, rain could have a big impact on a company's capacity to organise outdoor events. Checking the weather forecast is an early warning indicator that will help to prepare workarounds or completely shift the efforts (employees stay at home). Every business has some circumstances that have an impact on the overall performance, but these should not be taken for granted and abused as an excuse for non-performance. The root cause analysis should specify exactly what the correlation is between the circumstances and the performance. This correlation can be translated into an early warning indicator that can predict the impact of circumstances or work as a trigger to go for plan B.

ANALYSIS FOR STOP THE BLEEDING

This analysis focuses on root causes that are in between 'weakest link' and 'circumstances'. Stop the bleeding must be carried out when the analysis has shown that the root cause is beyond the control of employees, but not beyond the control of the entire organisation. The efforts made by employees so far are good and effective, but the overall result is still not in line with expectations. Therefore other departments within the organisation need to try to address the root cause.

A good example can be found in organisations that have many employees involved in data clean-up – that is, approaching existing customers to update their contact details. If the initial process of data capturing for new customers was not changed, or if the database is still not protected from edits by unauthorised employees, then it is likely that the clean-up project will never be completed. The root cause of low employee performance is caused by poor execution or poor support elsewhere in the organisation. The challenge, therefore, is to stop the bleeding before further efforts are made.

ANALYSIS FOR QUICK WINS

The last root cause analysis is aimed at finding quick wins. Change is mostly hard, and if progress is limited despite all efforts seemingly being done correctly, then it makes sense to look for quick wins.

> *Small successes can help to keep the spirit high and encourage people to continue doing the right things.*

Quick wins can be achieved by focusing on 'low-hanging fruit'. These are areas within the bigger assignment where relatively low effort will result in a relatively high impact.

If, for example, a new feature was developed based on certain customers' complaints, then it makes sense to approach these customers first to share the good news. The likely positive feedback will boost employees' motivation to offer the same solution to other customers. Quick wins can be found by asking staff what they felt went well and what they would like to replicate. Focusing on quick wins will create results for the organisation and build up employees' experience, which will create the self-confidence and momentum necessary to become even more successful.

The analysis block of care and control starts by getting a more in-depth understanding of the root causes that most influenced the outcome. From there, the aim is to assess the options of what can still be done and which action is likely to have the biggest impact. During analysis, it could make sense to not only look at what could be done more, better, different or less, but also readjust the action and/or result goals depending on what kind of outcome you are looking for.

Progress	• Kicked off activity as agreed?
Impact	• Achieved deliverables to see impact?
Analysis	• Root cause, best practice or lessons learned are clear?
Feedback	• Support and stretch for further growth and grooming?

Care & control

FEEDBACK

The aim of giving feedback as a manager is to stretch and groom employees and build their confidence. The MILL model specifies the four different ways of providing feedback. However, first, the manager should challenge/coach the employee to think for themselves which option could work for them. If nothing comes up, the manager should be able to find out which intervention works best for each employee.

Building confidence, stretching and grooming can be stimulated by the manager by using the following interventions

MOTIVATION	→	*WHY?*	Explaining benefits
INSPIRATION	→	*HOW?*	Sharing examples
STIMULATION	→	*WHAT?*	Giving suggestions
APPRECIATION	→	*IMPACT!*	Showing recognition

MANAGEMENT
MASTER MIND

CHAPTER 25

FEEDBACK

'Too often we give our children the answers to remember rather than the problem to solve.'

ROGER LEWIN

The last care and control activity to be initiated by the manager during the week is about feedback. Feedback is not a top-down assessment where a manager criticises and the staff member has to defend themselves. Such a set-up will not create a good learning environment in which feedback can be used for learning and grooming.

> *Feedback should always be constructive and therefore provide input for grooming and development.*

Even peers are encouraged to support each other in their learning by providing their views and suggestions on how colleagues can improve. Although the examples below refer to managers, they could also be used for peer feedback.

The MILL model encourages staff to take ownership for their own development, which starts with a self-assessment on their performance so far. After the employee has given their self-assessment, the manager can comment on the ideas generated by the employee on performance improvement (what can be done more, better, different or less). The manager can then add one or two observations of their own, without repeating what staff have already mentioned.

Feedback from the manager can be straightforward comments or appreciation for what has been achieved. It is, however, advisable to alternate this approach with some other ways of giving feedback, especially when further improvement or stretch is expected. In the paragraphs below, the added value will be described of some alternative ways for feedback, such as motivating, inspiring and stimulating. In this process of giving feedback to employees, the manager should build some understanding of what works best for each individual. Some employees will feel more engaged when they're given a better understanding of why their contribution is important for the organisation or themselves. Others are more likely to beef up their efforts when they get feedback in terms of sharing personal experience from the manager, or when they get inspired by a successful role model.

The following four methods detail the types of feedback a manager can give, which employees will most benefit, and in which situations they will be applicable.

MOTIVATION

Motivation is about the employees understanding and appreciating the benefits that achieving the goal will bring to themselves, the organisation or other stakeholders. The manager can support this process by explaining this added value and how even smaller steps in the process will, in the end, contribute to the overall outcome. The employee needs to understand why his work is important for the organisation and/or how he will benefit ('what's in it for me'). Motivation could be focused on short-term rewards, but it can also be about achieving a position (ambition), or a state, such as healthy or rich (aspiration), in the longer term.

> *Motivation is always about a perceived benefit, and the task of the manager is to create clarity on how the current activities will contribute to that desired benefit in the future.*

The manager may have to ask 'why' a few times to find out what really motivates employees.

- Why? '... because I can build experience.'
- Why? '... to take a bigger job one day.'
- Why? '... to earn more salary.'
- Why? '... because one day I want to design my own house!'

Motivating is also about supporting or strengthening ambition or aspiration to have a higher role one day. The manager may know what is required to achieve that goal, and staff will be happy to be stretched if they know that stretching will bring them closer to their dream job.

INSPIRATION

> *Employees can get inspired if they see how other people have achieved great results.*

Inspiration is often related to role models, which could range from family members to famous people. Inspiration comes, most of the time, from the achievements or attitude of these role models or a combination of both. People love to hear how somebody became successful despite difficult circumstances. It is important to check whether employees have such a person in mind – someone who is respected or admired – and which of the person's achievements or attitude they appreciate most. What did the role model do that could be translated to an action improvement for the employee in question?

In cases where employees do not have famous people whom they admire, the manager could also refer to colleagues or peers who can act as a role model. If a task that was perceived as impossible by the employee has been successfully completed by a colleague, therefore creating a best practice, the employee may find this to be very inspiring. Connecting staff who could use some inspiration, by teaming them up with experienced colleagues, will simultaneously create recognition and appreciation for the staff member who developed the best practice.

> *Inspiration is about role models giving direction on what has been done before, which will create the belief that it is possible to do whatever needs to be done.*

STIMULATION

The third way to supply feedback is through stimulation, which is a more directive management intervention in which the manager suggests things for the employee to do. Stimulation can be applied if staff have difficulty picking up new tasks or assignments. There may be lack of self-confidence, or they may lack the creativity required to explore what can be done differently or better, as committed to during the action improvement meeting. Motivation and inspiration do not provide enough support for these employees to jump the hurdle, or they may still have no clue about what could be done. In order to stimulate them, the manager needs to come up with suggestions and support the employee in deciding what will be tried.

Before stretching staff outside their comfort zone, the manager has to get a sense of what the perceived worst case is for the employee in terms of failure. These fears should be considered before applying stimulation, and the manager should make sure that people feel safe to 'experiment' in the suggested way. The action improvements that are suggested as stimulation are ideally based on best practices; this shows the employee that there is no reason for fear as the suggested approach really does work. Stimulation is about the employee making smaller, less risky steps, and at the same time the manager staying around for support and inspecting what is expected; if there is no follow-up, employees may shy away from the task. Stimulation gives clear direction and is focused on building self-confidence by making small steps with appropriate recognition.

APPRECIATION

Appreciation is the most important step to start and end any engagement, as appreciation is always constructive and supportive. Appreciations should be related to success, which can be either lessons learned or results achieved. Both are considered to be successes in the MILL model, therefore both should be appreciated, as long as the lessons learned are actionable for future improvements. Also exceptional efforts, a superb attitude or outstanding results that may not be directly related to committed action improvements, should be appreciated by the manager. Explaining how these examples have made the manager feel proud and happy is an excellent way to appreciate employees while reinforcing these important qualities.

Appreciation should focus on the process of the action improvements that created results, rather than the results themselves. When a manager recognises and appreciates efforts that have resulted in success, this generally provides more powerful feedback than simply rewarding the final outcome. Appreciation of individuals should be shared with the whole team, as it will send a message to the team about what the manager feels is important. Staff members can also be encouraged to share their mutual appreciation.

Care and control always requires feedback to grow and groom employees.

Feedback is breakfast for champions – it will not be clear without feedback how best to make progress. Feedback can give staff more direction, self-confidence, ambition and satisfaction, thus creating more eagerness and ownership.

The type of feedback that should be used best and how to alternate it depends on the specific challenges a staff member is facing. Feedback will always have a positive impact as long as it is constructive, forward-looking and encourages staff to explore opportunities.

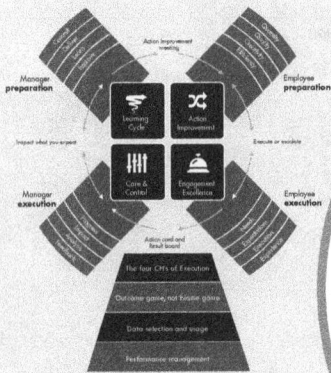

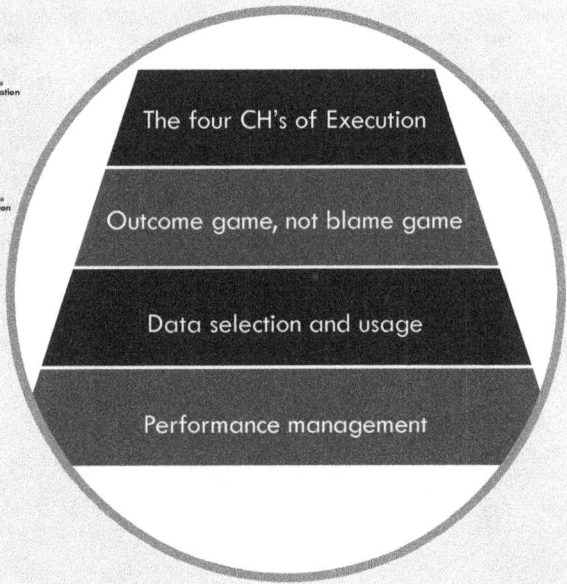

PART 7:
THE BASE OF
THE MILL MODEL:
MAKING IT WORK

This final part will explain what organisations can do or should have in place to support and stimulate the implementation of the model. There are four areas that will be discussed:

- **Execution**: This is the key skill for any organisation and some best practices are shared that will improve execution, provided that the manager owns and drives these recommendations.

- **Outcome-game**: This leadership style is the required approach for management to deal with set-backs and challenges. Sometimes the blame game can be counterproductive, and change may even slow down.

- **Data**: Knowledge is crucial for learning so there should be a thorough process of selecting and using data to make sure that the correct kind of changes are made and there is a growing understanding of what works best.

- **Performance**: Finally, there is also a need to leverage the potential of performance management, avoiding the pitfalls and combing performance management with consequence management to deal with all performance levels.

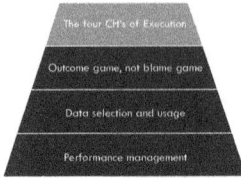

EXECUTION

	CHANGE	• Doing the same thing will lead to the same results • Management should also be capable and willing to change and reflect on their role to drive change
	CHOOSE	• Management has to understand the capacity and capability of employees to see what a realistic stretch is • It is important to make clear what is most important thus supporting employees in priority setting
	CHANNEL	• Channeling is about organizing and structuring data driven change in a predictable consistent manner • Proper processing of signals and data will avoid that there will be ad-hoc meetings and the team loses focus or gets confused on priorities
	CHEW	• Management should show the big picture but spend most time in translating observations in actions • Breaking down bigger assignments in smaller pieces will create an easier start and more speed than starting big

CHAPTER 26

EXECUTION

'Action is the foundational key to all success.'

PABLO PICASSO

The next four chapters will describe, from different angles, what makes people in an organisation move, but also what pitfalls and challenges can be expected when implementing the principles described in this book. The MILL model is mostly focused on daily operations, but some additional concepts need to be endorsed throughout the organisation to make it work.

This part's first chapter of 'making it work' is about execution. Execution is where the rubber hits the road. This is where it all should happen, and is often the most difficult part of the process because this is where the talking is over and both manager and employee have to start acting on their knowledge.

> **All the theory, the reports, the books read and the meetings held are useless until the knowledge gained and decisions made are implemented.**

Execution is where the real change or improvement has to happen. The challenge is that, in general, people are willing to change themselves but are reluctant to be changed by others. Management therefore has a duty to have employees involved in the process of 'change, choose, channel and chew'. These four concepts are at the core of execution and reinforce the MILL model to create empowerment and accountability.

CHANGE

Management is both the driver and the owner of change. Managers should therefore also exercise self-reflection and try to improve themselves if the approach used to get the best out of employees is not working.

> **Managers who wonder why staff are still not doing what they expect them to do should look in the mirror and will probably have to change their own approach.**

If there is no willingness or capability to change and the managers keep pushing in the same way again and again, only harder and harder, this will probably have a negative impact on the quality, diversity and self-confidence of the team. In this situation good people walk away, clones of the manager stay, and everybody gets nervous about the next push. Staff could respond by becoming reactive or passive, thinking 'Fine, have it your way,' and start sabotaging and undermining the organisational goals by playing hide and seek and spending more time on politics than performance.

Management that shows the capacity and willingness to change itself, and contributes to the improvements required from employees, will motivate teams much more. This is the best practice of leading by example. Ideas for areas where management could improve can be collected by encouraging staff to give feedback and suggestions. For example, asking for opinions on why meetings or follow-up are not always effective and efficient can provide input for the managers' self-reflection. It will set the right tone – of learning by doing – and the quality of staff feedback can also be used to identify those with management potential. Some staff may have great ideas for improvement that show their capability to think beyond their own responsibility.

CHOOSE

It is recommended that the change process starts by the manager having an understanding of the employees' capacity and capability to change by checking experience and workload. Even activities that can save time once executed, may have to be practised, and may require a bit more time to implement, so management has to choose which activities to start with. Good initiatives can fail and be deemed unsuccessful if insufficient time is allocated to develop the concept. Staff and management will never 'get the time' to do something new and improve unless they 'make the time'. Therefore it may be necessary to shift tasks to other staff or allow certain activities to be parked for the time being, but the manager and employee must be in agreement about this.

Management has to be crisp clear on the priorities and choose to execute what is most important. It is well known that employees can be more productive if they have less variety of tasks and if they are happy in their job because there is empowerment and encouragement. A continuous stream of new ideas and new instructions from the manager will lower productivity, as staff tend to wait for the next idea to arrive and become confused about what is really important. This could result in an organisation that can act only when important issues become urgent, which will create a culture of permanent panic and chaos.

Allowing staff to address the important issues first and giving them ample time for proper execution is more efficient and puts less pressure on quality than just adding tasks and ultimately forcing staff to act only on urgencies. Any proposed change that comes on top of existing activities will automatically result in some other activity being dropped, and if a manager continues to add tasks on top of existing work, employees are likely to make their own decisions on the work they prefer to drop. Clear priorities will prevent the constant interruptions that stopping and starting activities creates. A clear management agenda will enable employees to organise their daily activities efficiently and apply batch processing where appropriate.

> **Only if management is clear in the choices to be made, then staff can be expected to properly plan their work.**

This won't happen if there are constant interruptions, many ad-hoc meetings and ongoing changes of direction.

CHANNEL

Channelling ensures that an organisation has a structure and process in place that enables it to 'digest' all the different signals that it is faced with (reactive signals) or is looking for (proactive signals). It does not make sense, for example, to start a (proactive) customer satisfaction survey if there is no structure and process in place for dealing with the report once it comes out. There should be some understanding upfront of how the follow-up will be done and how digesting the outcome and recommendations into actions will be channelled. Channelling also means that there is consistent tracking and tracing of the action plan after digesting the signals and translating them into actions.

It is the manager's responsibility to streamline the process of channelling and digesting all the different signals into one coherent action plan, with due consideration given to the conditions of change (how is the manager going to contribute?) and choose (what else will be stopped or postponed), as described before. The manager could, for example, set up a weekly or monthly meeting structure that can accommodate all the different signals that have been received. Some members of the team should be identified to do some upfront homework and share recommendations in the meeting. The meeting should focus on decision making, and information that is not relevant to that will not be discussed.

CHEW

Chewing is another effort that management can make to accommodate staff in the change process. Chewing refers to the breaking down of large assignments, which require more time to complete, into 'bite-sized' smaller action points that can start immediately and therefore achieve results much quicker. Even a long journey of a thousand miles will, in the end, only be successful if small steps are made every single day. Climbing a mountain is easier when walking at a slow, steady pace than when running and resting in turn.

For bigger and more complex assignments, it is worth remembering that you can go faster if you slow down.

To get a new activity started, the bar should not be too high. The first steps should be smaller and therefore easier to achieve to get employees ahead of the schedule and create a positive, can-do attitude. Big changes never happen overnight, and building confidence is required to develop resilience for possible future setbacks. To facilitate the process of chewing, it can make sense to split priorities in three categories:

- Prio 1: Ready to 'eat' – actions for the coming (two) weeks.

- Prio 2: Being cooked, but not ready yet – actions are expected to take place in the next two to four weeks, but there is some uncertainty/dependency.

- Prio 3: The ingredients that will be cooked in the future.

During meetings, limited time should be spent on Prio 2 and even less on Prio 3. Once Prio 2 becomes Prio 1, more time can be spent on what needs to be done and what is expected. Chewing requires the manager to be quite firm, as employees love to talk about issues that do not require their actions. The manager must ensure everyone stays focused on Prio 1 which are actions that can and will be executed in the next two weeks.

Change, choose, channel and chew are essential tools for execution and should be used in combination. All four are focused on immediate action rather than long discussions with no clear outcome. Although all of them may look obvious, it may be difficult to implement them, as organisations often develop unproductive habits over time that require discipline and persistence, to change.

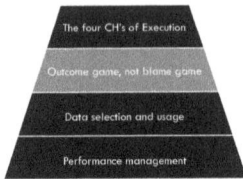

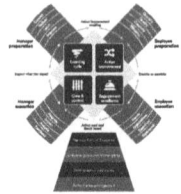

OUTCOME GAME, NOT BLAME GAME

☹ BLAME GAME	OUTCOME GAME ☺
What happened?	What happened?
How could it have happened?	How could we avoid that to happen again?
What damage do we have?	What benefit will we have in that case?
Who should have done something?	Who could support us to achieve this?
Why did they did not act?	When and where can we start?
... WHO IS TO BLAME?	.. WHAT OUTCOME ARE WE LOOKING FOR?
And nothing is changing...	And staff will start running...
Because we cannot change the past	Because we can change our future

PAST   FUTURE

← —— TIME —— →

CHAPTER 27

THE OUTCOME GAME, NOT BLAME GAME

'A man can fail many times, but he isn't a failure until he begins to blame somebody else.'

JOHN BURROUGHS

Many change programs fail or are only partially successful, even when it seems that all steps and recommendations have been followed. This can result in big losses, or at least some time lost and fruitless efforts, and leave staff feeling frustrated. And after a failed change effort, asking employees to participate in a new change program for a second time will be even harder.

So why do quite a few change management programs only have limited success? One of the main reasons is that despite the good intentions, many change programs focus only on what should be done instead of also covering what should be stopped. Of course, stopping some of the existing activities is important to make time for new activities. But it is even more important to identify, and stop, activities that could be counter-productive to the goal you want to achieve under the change program.

> *If you want to accelerate your car, you'll be told that you have to push the throttle, but it is equally important to release the break.*

Implementing change under the MILL model therefore also requires some awareness of the culture, structures or processes in an organisation that could hinder successful implementation. Imagine, for example, a manager who has implemented the action improvement meeting to engage and empower employees and get their buy-in and ownership for proposed changes. If the senior manager he is reporting to continues with his or her directive leadership style – always giving detailed instructions that need to be obeyed without discussion – then it is unlikely that the goal of creating a learning organisation will be achieved. Another example is related to the culture in an organisation in which performance is not considered relevant to promotion. If employees have, so far, been promoted based on their education, their age or their relationship with senior management, then it is highly unlikely that a high performance culture will be achieved without changing the process for career development.

If implementing the MILL model is not as successful as expected, employees can be asked for their thoughts on what could be done better or differently outside the program itself. The most obvious reasons for low staff involvement (described in previous chapters) are the manager's failure to empower employees (poor implementation of the model) and to show enough care (see also motivation, inspiration, stimulation and appreciation in Chapter 25). Poor usage of performance management is another reason, which will be discussed in Chapter 29. One of the most common pitfalls for successful change, which we will discuss in this chapter, is related to the way management deals with setbacks and failures.

> *Many organisations have the tendency to find someone to blame for failure, rather than working out what can be done to improve the situation.*

Every organisation will have situations where performance is too low, systems break down, customers complain or other issues are concerning. In those situations, management can respond in two ways. These options are called the 'blame game' and the 'outcome game'. The outcome game is supportive and aligned with the approach under the MILL model, but the blame game is the opposite and can ruin all efforts to build a learning organisation. This chapter will explain why and how playing the blame game should be replaced with playing the outcome game.

THE BLAME GAME

Imagine a situation where management has discovered that, due to human error, the delivery of goods was delayed for a whole week and caused a considerable loss for the company. Under the blame game approach, management will try to dig deeper on exactly what happened, why it happened and who was involved. Did somebody do something wrong? Was somebody negligent? In this situation, all stakeholders can sense that management is looking for somebody to blame. This leads to employees showing all kinds of defensive responses.

Staff will look for something or somebody else to blame, or hide themselves behind technical language and other 'smoke and mirrors'. Finding out for certain who is to blame and, if multiple employees are involved, what the 'ranking' of the blame is, can be a time-consuming process for management. Employees involved will continue to defend themselves, putting the cooperation and mutual support within the team under pressure. During this time of confusion and tension, it is likely that there will be limited attention on mitigating the risk of the same thing happening again.

Everybody agrees that it should not have happened, but employees realise that suggesting a solution could make somebody a suspect – management could respond to a suggested solution by questioning why that idea was not executed before disaster struck. This kind of denial makes solving the real issue a burden and the blame game will undermine any effort to build a learning organisation under the MILL model.

THE OUTCOME GAME

The outcome game has the same starting position as the blame game – management wants to understand what has happened.

> *The intention here, however, is not to blame somebody, but to find out what can be learned and what can be done to avoid similar issues happening again.*

There will be an appeal to staff to come up with ideas (action improvements) on how to manage the situation better in the future by checking what can be monitored and who can provide support. Management is clear that they do not expect anybody to be able to change the past. That does not mean that there is low accountability, but employees will be held accountable for solutions for the future instead of problems in the past that cannot be changed anymore.

The questions that should be asked under the outcome-game, are always forward looking, after the root-cause is understood:

• How could we avoid this to happen again?

• What benefit will we have in that case ?

- Who could support us to achieve this ?

- When and where can we start ?

This approach will create more team involvement and faster results. Going forward, accountability will be stronger, as it will be much clearer what could go wrong and who is supposed to do what in such a situation. The team can agree on early warning indicators that will be monitored and back-up systems or other workarounds that will be kept on stand-by. The team has learned a valuable lesson, and realises that next time failure could have serious consequences for the individuals who are accountable. However, after playing the outcome game, it is crystal clear what will be done to avoid repetition as employees will team up to find solutions rather than pointing fingers.

The blame game is about the past, while the outcome game is about the future. Nobody can change the past, so even if playing the blame game results in finding the culprit, that does not mean that the issue will not happen again.

> Punishing employees by blaming could work counter-productive to finding and implementing a solution

The outcome game creates true accountability by engaging with the staff involved and letting them take ownership for the solutions they have developed.

Change management programs are not only about doing the right things, but also about not doing the wrong things. As long as the organisation continues playing the outcome game and looks for solutions to overcome challenges, every obstacle that could block the implementation of the MILL model can be removed.

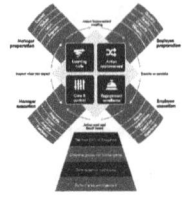

DATA SELECTION AND USAGE

Strategic data
- Opportunities and threats showing the big picture of development and direction
- Use for strategic plans and budgeting; (semi) annually

Tactical data
- Planning and dependencies to allocate responsibilities and create alignment
- Use to check whether still on track in terms of progress and direction; quarterly/monthly

Execution data
- Action and result goals in detail creating clarity to kick start execution
- For evaluating impact and lessons learned and action improvement; weekly

Control data
- Development taken place in compliance with rules, cost, etc.
- Ensuring that growth and development is sustainable; monthly

Most common pitfalls for data analysis and processing:

- *Poor analysis/ preparation of data before the meeting or not including a review of assumptions upfront results in data discussion during the meeting rather than focus on action commitment.*
- *Limited cascading or relating data to bigger organisational goals resulting in limited buy-in or sense of urgency due to lack of understanding bigger picture.*
- *More focus on short-term failures than positive trends and learning from both mistakes and successes, which results in limited or no action improvements.*
- *Unbalanced performance indicators resulting in unbalanced growth, continuous shifting goals and adjusting achievements.*

MANAGEMENT
MASTER MIND

CHAPTER 28:

DATA-SELECTION
AND USAGE

'The goal is to turn data into information,
and information into insights.'

CARLY FIORINA

This chapter aims at 'unpacking' data availability and data usage. By slicing and dicing the available data into 'bite-sized' pieces, it becomes easier to see what can be done with data, which data is not required and how to explore new sources of data.

> The current business environment supplies an overload of data that requires a more structured approach to select, filter, analyse and digest it all.

Under the MILL model, employees are encouraged to collect even more data, so it is very important to set priorities and have proper processing. If this doesn't happen, organisations will become very inefficient: they will produce more data than required; decision making may be based on the wrong data; and decisions may be postponed because confusion has been created by having to go through too much or poorly prepared data.

The challenges that need to be addressed are:

- **Selecting data:** Start with the goal of the analysis and what question should be answered, to become aware what data could be relevant. A common pitfall is that there is limited upfront thinking and understanding of what data is required in terms of decision making or action improvement and just use whatever is available.

> *In today's environment, there are hardly any limitations to accessing date, so do not limit yourself to only the data that are readily available.*

- **Filtering data:** Check what the quality of the available data is, what can be used to determine direction to drive behaviour (what to do), and what can be used to determine conditions to guide behaviour (what to watch). For example, financial reports on profit and loss and balance sheets generally do not indicate what to do, although they can indicate that action is required. Market share reports can better indicate where action is required.

- **Analysing data:** The selected data should be used to analyse patterns and correlations, leading to understanding of root causes. It has been described in Chapter 24 that analysis can be done by comparing results with the plan, the trend, peers and impact. Analysis should make it clear what action is likely to result in the highest impact and therefore which action improvements to prioritise. If you do not know which button to push, pushing them all does not make sense.

- **Implementing data:** Implementing data means that it is clear how data are used for decision making on action. The expected results are also captured for tracking and tracing and future validation of the impact of actions taken. Data will be used for action and result goals, and the outcome of the effort will be used to check whether the correct data was used and the correct assumptions were made.

In short, there needs to be an understanding why data is needed and how data will be used. It should be clear to all stakeholders how the variety of data can be linked to the process, from the strategic/tactical level to execution and control.

DATA CATEGORIES

Different categories of data are suitable for different types of decision making. Selecting and filtering data starts with grouping all available data into four categories and thereafter having different engagement structures in place to analyse and digest these different categories of data.

- **Strategic data:** This category of data will provide information required for making decisions about the direction a company wants to go in the long run. It considers trends in the organisation's strengths and weaknesses in relation to opportunities and threats in the environment. Strategic data are used to give clarity on where the organisation wants to be in three to five years. Examples are inflation, market share, GDP growth or other macro-economic and sector-specific trends.
  → Needed for the annual budget discussion, as it requires discussion and decision making from senior management. Thereafter it is required quarterly to track progress and protect direction.

- **Tactical data:** This category of data will provide information required to make plans and allocate responsibilities. The journey towards the strategic direction of the organisation has to be broken down into milestones and split into accountabilities related to internal capacity and capabilities. Tactical data will show whether the organisation is on track so far, and whether the various stakeholders contribute in line with expectation. Examples are financial budgets, distribution plans, marketing plans and so forth.

→ Evaluated by all management levels on a monthly to quarterly basis to define or realign plans for the next month or quarter, based on the outcome of the previous quarter.

- **Execution data:** Once there is clarity on the plan, it should become clear what data is required to keep track of progress. These data also provide input for the learning and improving process, such as monitoring action improvement, action and result goals. Execution data is often developed within a department to track what needs to be done or what needs to be adjusted. Examples are sales reports, campaign plans, action cards and result boards.

  → Weekly data to check what productivity and progress levels have been achieved in the previous week. It shows whether execution of the plan is on track and where the team can learn and improve.

- **Control data:** To meet the conditions set or to check whether the organisation is within the approved framework, data that can provide information on compliance with internal and external rules and regulations is required. Control data are used as early warning indicators for potential side effects of stretching the organisation. Examples are financial indicator reports, risk reports, compliance reports and so forth.

  → Discussed in monthly meetings by finance and control departments to see whether quality or compliance has been jeopardised by stretching performance.

Mixing these brackets of data may create confusion, as they all have a different added value. For example, if reports with strategic data have been put on the agenda during a progress meeting on execution but the strategic decision makers are not attending, then proceeding with strategic discussions will be a waste of time. By defining these four brackets, it becomes clear that discussing each type of data requires a different audience, different timing and different purpose.

USING DATA EFFECTIVELY

Under the MILL model, the focus will be on execution data, while other data will be forwarded to the appropriate meeting as specified above. Analysing and digesting the available data can also be done in a more effective manner by applying the following recommendations:

- **No ongoing data-quality discussions**
  Discussions on the reliability of data should be restricted to once or twice a year. It is very unproductive if employees keep arguing the validity and integrity of data. Even if the starting point may be arguable, trends still show progress, and impact and comparison among peers is still possible. If there are seasonal or other patterns that are used as an excuse to explain gaps, this explanation comes too late as these could and should already have been incorporated in the budget. Data should be presented in such a way that it indicates conclusions that can inform decision making. It should not create confusion resulting in lengthy discussions or would first require extensive clarification.

Employees should be challenged to see how the insights provided by the data can be used instead of discussing what is missing.

- **Cascade data to values and strategic goals**

  Organisational values, for example eagerness, ownership and the organisation's strategic goals, can be cascaded down to departmental key performance indicators (KPIs) and even individual KPIs. By doing this, it will become clear to all staff how they are not only expected to contribute to the organisational performance goal, but also how the expected behaviour and results will be measured. The value of eagerness could be measured in terms of new initiatives and the value of ownership could be measured by giving quality scores on the work delivered. This kind of goal alignment will strengthen both the team spirit and individual motivation as it becomes clearer what the importance of everybody's role is for the overall growth of the organisation.

- **Look at what is good and what is on trend**

  When analysing data, there is a tendency to look at concerns and failures to understand what needs to be done to improve, but this focus on weaknesses (or the 'red' category) can result in a more defensive response from staff. It could well be, however, that more lessons can be learned from strengths (or the 'green' category), as this is where the drivers for success can be found that could also be applied to overcome challenges. A similar shift of focus can be applied by paying more attention to trends rather than status (see also Chapter 23).

> *A good direction is more important than the historic position.*

A market leader that is losing market share has a bigger problem than the second-ranked competitor that is growing its market share.

- **Look at the big picture**

  Sustainable growth can only be achieved if there is balanced growth, which implies that there is a need to assess data on developments from a number of different angles. Pushing the sales numbers but failing to monitor risks and claims could backfire one day, as there was insufficient attention given to the conditions for growth. Conditions for growth should also include staff and customer satisfaction, as no long-term success can be expected without happy staff and loyal customers, hence the ForYou/4U customer satisfaction check as part of Engagement excellence (see Chapter 21).

The MILL model is aiming for data-driven change, but searching for even more data means that there should be a constant review of the available data and how they are being used in order to avoid data overload. Discussing the quality of data in a meeting should be avoided, because these discussions may not be very fruitful as they tend to take longer than decision making. Therefore, only relevant and reliable data should be presented in a meeting. By having an upfront idea of what data is required and having different platforms to process different categories of data, the whole organisation can benefit. Data-driven change implies that data is only shared if it will be used to direct the discussion, guide the decision making and monitor implementation and impact.

PERFORMANCE MANAGEMENT

Employee performance so far. (vertical axis)

- - - average - - -

Clearly above average

Around average

Below average-clearly improving

Below average-hardly moving

OPENING MESSAGE:	OPENING MESSAGE:	OPENING MESSAGE:	OPENING MESSAGE:
Is it clear what was expected and what else could be the problem	*Recognise good efforts and progress made so far*	*Well done & appreciated so recognition for effort and result*	*Well done if outcome is related to effort, understand best practice*
CHALLENGE:	**CHALLENGE:**	**CHALLENGE:**	**CHALLENGE:**
Serious effort and clear change expected	*More analysis on impact required; still more effort required or change approach*	*Challenge for stretch, referring to highest performers, more options to be explored*	*Repeat and improve best practice, share and support colleagues*

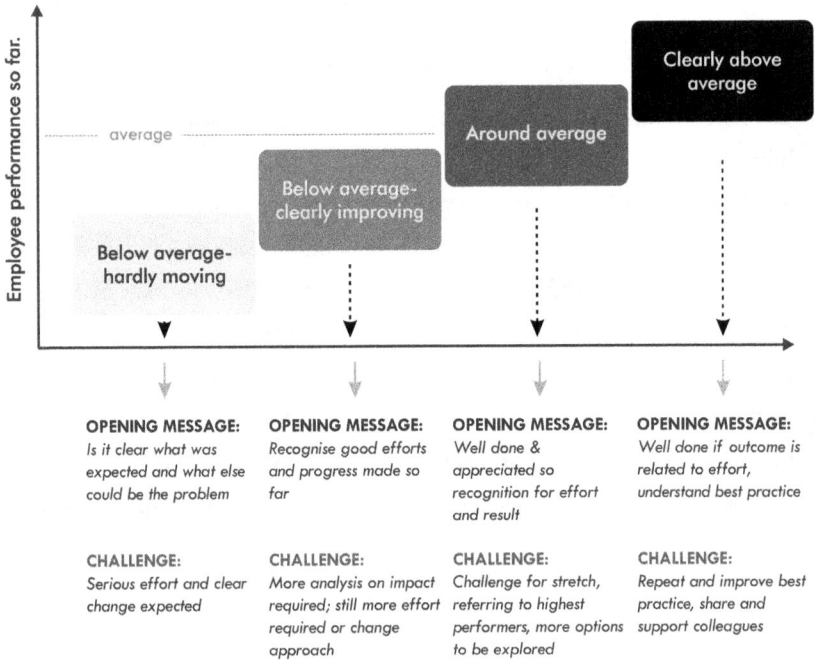

MANAGEMENT
MASTER MIND

CHAPTER 29

PERFORMANCE MANAGEMENT

'Employees become more valuable when they
are more valued.'

ARJAN MOLENKAMP

Embedding and consistently driving performance management throughout the organisation is crucial to create a performance-oriented culture that supports the MILL model by recognition and rewarding both efforts and results.

> *If there is no supporting structure to show that action improvements will, in the end, also somehow benefit to the individual, employees may feel that management does not really care.*

Performance management is, however, not the same as offering bonuses or profit sharing; there is a whole range of other instruments that can be used to recognise and reward employees. Nor should performance management be an exercise initiated by the human resources department that only gets management attention twice a year. Embedding it into the culture will require ongoing attention and the manager should take full ownership of the process. Performance management should go hand-in-hand with consequence management, which is the other side of the coin in which management not only pays attention to exceptionally high performance but, in the same structured fashion, also pays attention to exceptionally low performance, a breach, negligence or other poor behaviour.

Performance management under the MILL model has two dimensions.

1. Recognition for outstanding efforts.
   - Recognition is verbal and/or symbolic.
   - Efforts are outstanding compared to peer or previous performance and in line with model behaviour (values).

1. Rewarding exceptional results created by outstanding efforts.
   - Rewarding is done by a more material/financial incentive.
   - Exceptional results means far beyond targets and peers, but also balancing various KPIs for sustainable growth.
   - Outstanding performance means action improvements beyond targets and peers.

The intention of performance management is to not only show appreciation for exceptional results, but also show that management cares by recognising outstanding efforts.

RECOGNITION VERSUS REWARD

Recognition is related to outstanding efforts and can be done throughout the year in many ways, but never in cash. Outstanding efforts do not always lead to exceptional results, so it would not be appropriate to give extra money if the company is not making extra money. Recognition can be done by putting somebody in the spotlight, offering to take them to lunch or dinner, introducing them to top management personnel, offering a professional development course, or presenting them with a tangible token that is visible to peers, family and friends (certificate, trophy, badge, etc.). Recognition is used to openly show the team what is perceived by management as an example of good attitude and behavioural change, and that these are appreciated by management. This should encourage other staff to start exploring how they can make the same outstanding efforts.

> **Rewarding is related to exceptional results but only if these are created by outstanding efforts.**

Rewarding is generally only done once or twice a year, as the results should be sustainable and not based on one or two lucky shots. Only the top ten to twenty per cent of performers are likely to qualify for these kinds of rewards, and the results must be both exceptionally better than that of their peers and exceed budget targets. If most staff have exceeded budget targets, rewards should only be given to the top 10-20 % performers, as the targets were obviously too low. It is important that employees that qualify for this kind of reward also have acceptable minimum levels of both work quality and teamwork to make sure that results and behaviour are sustainable and balanced.

THE TRADITIONAL APPROACH

The traditional performance management approach, as still applied in many organisations, is far less effective than the recommendations under the MILL model. The following example will clarify:

Imagine a stockbroking department during the internet hype of the year 2000. Sales consultants guide customers on which stock to buy and, as every stock went up that year, the sales consultants easily persuaded customers to buy the recommended stocks and they all exceeded their targets. Everybody got their bonus. But the next year the internet bubble burst and customers just wanted to sell, or were sending claims for the poor advice they received the year before. The sales consultants had never had to work so hard to protect the organisation against big losses, but none of the budgets were achieved and nobody got a bonus.

How can it be that one year everybody is an excellent employee, and the year after nobody is any good? Could it be that in the first year some employees exceeded the budget considerably more than others, but without management recognition? Could it be that in both years some employees showed more effort than others? Why should management not recognise the hard work in the second year? This is not performance management, but rather profit sharing. There was no attention given for exceptional results based on outstanding efforts, only attention for results, and even that analysis was not fair to some employees who were outperforming relative to their peers.

The consequence of this type of management is that employees sense a lack of care and recognition from management. They will stop trying to do better than their peers and get better at their jobs, as circumstances have a bigger impact than their own efforts on whether they will be rewarded.

PERFORMANCE MANAGEMENT UNDER THE MILL MODEL

The manager has an important role to play in motivating and encouraging employees to become better. Most organisations have employee personal development plans as part of the annual appraisal process. Instead of one annual review, it makes sense to have more frequent but smaller reviews, aiming for more gradual and consistent personal development. If the employee's capabilities can be stretched beyond the current job requirements to prepare for the next step, the manager has to provide support by breaking down bigger assignments into bite-size pieces. Monthly plans and evaluations during one-on-one sessions can be used to track progress and provide relevant feedback.

By scheduling time for monthly development feedback and making it a priority, the manager will maintain motivated employees who will be continuously improving.

Under the MILL model, there are four different categories of intervention under performance management. Which one should be used depends on the situation. Let's look at the four possible scenarios:

- **Below average performance**
  Staff with below average performance may have been trying hard, but have challenges related to the clarity of their assignment, their capability to perform it, the way they prepared for it or their attitude towards it. The manager has to find the root cause and staff should show awareness and commitment for action improvement. There could be legacy issues of demotions or they may be close to retirement but, whatever the case, poor performance needs to be addressed for two compelling reasons.

Success quadrant

Are you in the driving seat for success?

CLARITY: *The Map Plan*	▶	Do you know what you are looking for, what is required and what can be expected during the journey or the moment you arrive?
CAPABILITY: *The Engine*	▶	Do you have the skills, knowledge and support to make sure you can be successful?
ATTITUDE: *The Focus*	▶	Is it clear why you are doing this and are you committed to become successful whatever it takes?
PREPARATION: *The Fuel and Tyre Pressure*	▶	Are you well prepared in terms of people planning and tools on stan by to deal with every situation that can be expected

The first reason to challenge staff is that there should always be a management effort before somebody can be qualified as a poor performer and enter the process for consequence management. The second reason for putting the spotlight on low performers is to motivate high performers. If a manager accepts under-performance within a team, it will become very hard to stretch and challenge other team members who are already performing at a higher level.

High achievers are sensitive to non-performers who 'slow down the team' and expect management to intervene. High performers may reduce efforts or leave the company if the manager cannot address the performance challenges of individuals.

- **Below average performance but improving**

  Employees who are performing below average, but who have tried hard and made some improvements, should get some recognition for those improvements. A pitfall for a manager is to ignore the employee's efforts because they are not yet paying off and performance is still below average. However, if there is no positive feedback from management on the progress and impact of new behaviour, even if that progress and impact is small, these employees may quickly give up and slip back to their previous, lower performance levels.

  Underperforming staff who are seriously working on getting better probably have to put more effort into their job and show more stretch than average or even high performers. Performance management under the MILL model will not only look at the overall achievement versus budget by year-end, but also what efforts and performance improvement have been made to become better

- **Average performance**

  These employees generally believe that they are doing a pretty good job. During performance management engagement, they tend to limit their focus to areas where they have performed above average, even if their overall performance is around average. The manager has to be strong here by explaining that exceptional rewards are only applicable to exceptional results across the board, and while their performance is well appreciated, it is still about average. Being strict and only rewarding top performers is crucial, otherwise the whole purpose of performance management will be diluted. There are two important messages that the average performer needs to hear to make sure that they remain motivated and continue to show eagerness and ownership for improvement.

The first message is that average is well done and good because it is at par, and although it is not exceptional, their efforts are appreciated; targets will always make them stretch and they did well to meet the target. Their salary is the reward for doing what they are doing and what they are supposed to do, which is meeting targets. A round average performance does not imply that the staff member is considered to be an average person, but that their pretty steep performance is in line with the pretty steep expectations the organisation has.

The second message that needs to be made clear to these staff is specifying what the gap is between their performance and efforts and that of their peers who have shown outstanding efforts leading to exceptional results. It should be made clear what effort and outcome is expected from the average performer to move to the highest bracket. However, no exact definition of outstanding performance can be given, because the following year the best performers are likely to get better and therefore raise the bar even higher.

Outperformance under the MILL model is not based on outperformance of the budget, but outperformance of peers.

- **Clearly above average performance**

  This may look like the easiest category to provide recognition for, as it seems only required to provide a positive message without detailed discussions, but that is not the correct approach. Even for this category, it should be made clear that new outstanding efforts and exceptional results are required every year to stay on top. It should be made clear that the average performers are expected to raise the bar, which implies that simply continuing to do what has been done so far may not be sufficient. There are also two essential messages for this particular group.

  The first message is to explicitly recognise how exceptional efforts have resulted in exceptional outcomes or, in other words, what has been the impact of their role model attitude and behaviour. Financial rewards will not have an impact on continuous action improvements if the manager is not able to highlight the behaviour that contributed most to results.

> *Like any compliment, the more it can be substantiated, the more credible the compliment.*

The second message for outperformers is to give them some constructive feedback on areas for further improvement. High performers may get lazy or move to another company if they believe they have reached their ceiling and cannot (or do not have to) develop themselves further. More care for further personal development and stretching of high performers will have the biggest impact on overall performance of the team, as high performers generally make the biggest contribution to the overall team result.

Performance management is not easy, but once the manager understands the difference between reward and recognition and can group employees in the four categories of performance, then it becomes clear what feedback should be given to each category. Under the MILL model, consequence management and encouragement is just as important as financial rewarding in order to give the right signals to employees in support of their personal development.

CONCLUSION

LEARNING CYCLE

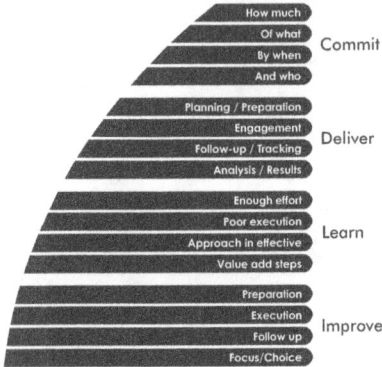

	Commit
How much	
Of what	
By when	
And who	

Deliver
- Planning / Preparation
- Engagement
- Follow-up / Tracking
- Analysis / Results

Learn
- Enough effort
- Poor execution
- Approach in effective
- Value add steps

Improve
- Preparation
- Execution
- Follow up
- Focus/Choice

ACTION IMPROVEMENT

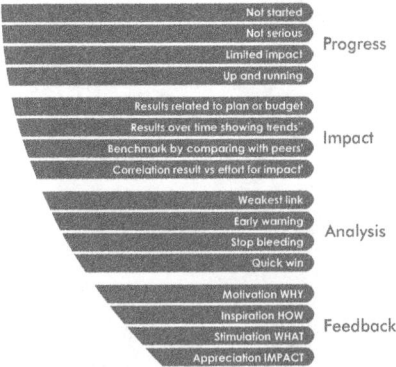

Quantity
- More often
- More time
- More Extended
- More focus

Quality
- Engagement
- Personal Skills
- Facilitation
- Attitude

Creativity
- How engaged
- What offered
- Which marketing P's
- Relationship management

Efficiency
- Time Wasting at Meetings
- Low Added Value Activities
- Service Level Agreement / Support
- Priority Setting by Management

Progress
- Not started
- Not serious
- Limited impact
- Up and running

Impact
- Results related to plan or budget
- Results over time showing trends"
- Benchmark by comparing with peers'
- Correlation result vs effort for impact"

Analysis
- Weakest link
- Early warning
- Stop bleeding
- Quick win

Feedback
- Motivation WHY
- Inspiration HOW
- Stimulation WHAT
- Appreciation IMPACT

Needs
- Future state
- Future Emotion
- Executing difference
- Interaction

Expectations
- Deliverable
- Process
- Dependencies
- Engagement

Execution
- Usage/benefits
- Progress Communication
- Specific wishes
- Differentiator

Experience
- End Product
- Process
- Competitive
- Follow Up

CARE & CONTROL

ENGAGEMENT CYCLE

MANAGEMENT
MASTER MIND

CONCLUSION

'Learning is the discipline of repeating without repetition.'

ARJAN MOLENKAMP

Changing, growing and developing from the lessons we learn is a natural part of the human condition. The evidence for this can be seen in many scenarios.

When a child is about one year's old, something special will happen. Holding on to a chair, the baby will raise itself to a standing position. You can see the baby's eyes looking at the couch where you are sitting and back to the chair. You can see that some plans are being developed in the baby's head. As a parent you act immediately by speaking encouraging words and stretching your arms out as an invitation. And then the miracle happens as the baby starts walking its first real steps towards you! As a parent you applaud and cheer and show recognition of how proud you are on this first attempt and the baby is smiling from ear to ear! The second thing that you will do is push the chair a bit further and challenge the baby to repeat the exercise, but now with one more step. The baby falls, but you will pick him or her up and compliment the child for the attempt, creating confidence that efforts are appreciated and support will always be available.

This book encourages management to use a similar approach when grooming employees. Management has a responsibility to encourage staff to make small steps. While they do this they will not be held, but will be supported. Employees are allowed to fail and once they succeed the results will be celebrated, but there will also be new assignments for further learning. There is a belief that, as a manager, you have a duty to groom and develop your employees and that they have the potential to learn and grow to higher levels.

Babies learn eagerly and naturally, but when children get older their parents have to employ new techniques to help them learn. Imagine having ten children, all of whom have their own room that is supposed to be cleaned every evening before dinner. You make it clear that you will inspect the cleaning one week from today. When will they start cleaning their room? Today? Tomorrow? Probably not. It is likely that they will clean their room just before you check it. It's normal to give lower priority to activities we're asked to do without a clear reason. Now imagine that you believe you have found the solution to the room-cleaning problem – daily statistics showing the percentage of rooms that have been cleaned. During dinner, you decide to share these statistics that show that only four out of ten rooms were cleaned. You urge the children to improve that number to become ten out of ten. So will it change now? Not likely, as no names were shared. Those children who cleaned their room did not get any recognition, and they wonder why they should continue being good. The ones who did not clean their rooms were not singled out either, and since it was not clear who failed and what the consequence would be for long-term failure, they will not bother to start cleaning their rooms. The 'cleaning score' could even go down, as the 'cleaners' may stop due to lack of recognition. The way for a parent to change this situation would be to 'inspect what they expect', as described in this book.

If change is required, some physical inspection of what is expected must be done to show care and control. It is important that performance is monitored and numbers are shared, but assessment should go beyond team performance – there is also a need to zoom in on an individual level. Making generic statements should be avoided, and instead it should be made clear what efforts and results are expected for each individual. Good results should also be recognised and appreciated to make sure others can learn and the good performance will expand.

Babies learn naturally, children can be encouraged to learn, and adults also benefit from the right sort of coaching. Amateur football players practise during the week and matches are played on the weekend. Before the match, the team sits down with the coach to analyse the opponent. The team will try to understand the challenges of winning the match as all players know the team's ranking and what the team's ambition is. Good ideas are brought up by the players and it is agreed what position every individual will play and how the strikers will be assisted. During half time, the team meets again to see how the first half went and what could be improved in the second half. Is there an opportunity to aim for more shots on the goal or could the passing be better? Some players agree to play a different position, and the defence players to move less in order to stay in the back and be better prepared for counters. If the match is won, the team celebrates the victory, but if they lose, another assessment is done to see where a difference could have been made. If a free kick was missed twice, then the whole team will practise the free kick during the week to make sure it's a strength during the next match.

This book encourages management to use a similar approach for creating a team and aim for continuous learning. Employees should understand the overall ambition of the organisation and come up with their ideas to contribute. Employees are committed to execute what was agreed and there will be engagements with the manager to identify areas for further action improvements if the results are not as expected. The manager acts as a coach by physically checking how the agreed tasks are being executed, and not relying only on the score board to see whether employees gave their best. Sometimes the achievements are still poor despite good efforts, but only by identifying and understanding the root causes can changes be made or renewed efforts practised. Successes are celebrated and all employees realise that they can achieve more as a team than the sum of the individual achievements.

This book has summarised these key learning concepts, that most of us understand instinctively and that we already apply, in such a way that they can also be used in the business environment. The guidance supplied in this book is not rocket science, but by making the critical steps more explicit, it will become easier to understand what is required to embed an interactive learning leadership style in any organisation.

Implementing the MILL model does not require a total rework of the organisation. The only thing that is required is a strong belief by management that employees have more potential, and will become more valuable, if they are more valued. Structure and discipline is required to make it work and to remain credible, management has to show staff that the new approach is really embraced. Management does not have to master all concepts of the MILL model from the start – the important thing is to show eagerness and ownership to reflect and to keep continuously improving, in line with what is expected from the employees.

On behalf of both myself and your employees, thank you very much for reading this book. You can make your employees and your organisation grow, and your customers happy, if you start working on the concepts shared in this book and, if possible ... start today! You may have to reread the book a few times, as some concepts require a bit more experience to implement, but it is worth all the effort. The most important person who will benefit from the success that you will create, beyond all the stakeholders mentioned above, is YOU!

CONGRATULATIONS!

For more information, further examples, and tools and recommendations that will guide you in using this book and implementing its advice, visit www.managementmastermind.com

GLOSSARY

Action card: Tracking document for the individual employee to capture commitment on actions and results. Execution of the action goals, as well as the outcome in terms of lessons learned or results, will be updated daily. The action card is used for self-reflection and for engagement with the manager to check progress and impact during the week, and is prepared immediately after the action improvement meeting.

Action goals: The action goal describes the activities that must take place to produce the expected results as committed during the action improvement meetings. Action goals are tracked by the employee on an action card and can be adjusted during the week after endorsement by the manager. Only by capturing both action and result goals and their outcome, the correlation between effort and impact can be measured, analysed and improved.

Action Improvement: This is the second 'blade' of the MILL model. It explains the four options for improvement, which always require some sort of action. Action improvements are new initiatives, suggested and selected by the employees themselves, to do something more, better, different or less. Actions and outcome will be tracked to assess the impact of the new behaviour and consider further action improvement.

Action improvement meeting (AIM): A weekly departmental meeting, organised and supported by the manager, to create employee commitment on both actions and results. Employees are empowered to come up with ideas for improvement, select the ideas to be actioned, and agree on action and result goals for endorsement by the manager. There are some strict rules that need to be followed to keep the meeting short, with high energy and broad involvement of all participants.

Blame game: Situation in which management is trying to find a culprit to blame for a loss or a problem. This approach does not solve the problem and makes employees fearful of taking ownership of the challenges that need to be addressed. This is contrary to the forward-looking outcome game, in which solutions are explored and accountability created. See also Outcome game

Breach: This is the failure to stick to a commitment while also failing to inform the manager immediately when it becomes clear that an action commitment will not be met. Breaches will be tracked and will have consequences if they recur. Breaches undermine the value of the commitment made, and if the manager does not address staff with a poor attitude this can have a negative impact on the team-spirit. See also Execute or escalate

Care and control: This is the fourth and last blade of the MILL model, which explains how the manager is expected to engage with the employee. Employees should experience the manager's care and control when they execute their action commitments and/or use engagement excellence to keep moving and keep improving. The manager will check progress and impact, and assist in analysing or giving feedback tailored to the particular scenario.

Consequence management: The MILL model focuses on avoiding blame, creating accountability and learning lessons from mistakes. This approach is, however, not optional, and the manager must address employees that walk away from their responsibility and accountability (by, for example, not sticking to their commitment). A manager failing to address cases of poor attitude or continued under-performance can have a negative impact on the whole team; the manager is implicitly lowering the bar for all staff by not taking action against poorly performing individuals.

Conversation partners: More generic descriptions for colleagues, suppliers and other stakeholders beyond external customers. The principles of engagement excellence are universal as, for example, understanding needs and managing expectations should not be exclusive for customers but should also be applied broadly within and outside the organisation for good relationships and effective meetings.

Early warning indicators: Employees should focus on what can be influenced, and everything else should be considered circumstantial. If certain circumstances can have a big impact on results, then indicators should be identified for monitoring significant changes in these high impact circumstances. These triggers can indicate when an alternative approach or workaround should be applied.

Engagement excellence: This is the third blade of the MILL model and describes four steps for engagement with customers or conversation partners. To get a better understanding what is relevant from a customer perspective (outside-in), the N(EX)3 model should be used. The execution of the engagement will be guided by the ForYou/4U approach, which has four steps that are aligned with N(EX)3.

Engagement partner: This can be an internal customer or employee, an external customer or other stakeholder, or a supplier or any other party who has a connection with an organisation and therefore will need to engage with the organisation. Engagement partners all have needs and expectations that must be met and/or exceeded and successful engagement is crucial for a high performing organisations.

Escalate: If action commitments by the employees cannot be met for whatever reason, the manager should immediately be made aware. Ownership for solving the challenge will remain at the employee level, but the manager can give recommendations and support. Escalation is not about blame gaming, but about managing expectations. It is not acceptable for a manager to not be made aware that action commitments are not going to be met. See Execute or escalate

Execute or escalate: Building a high-performance organisation requires transparency on the execution of commitment. Either employees stick to their commitment and execute as promised, or they inform the manager that commitments are unlikely to be met. There is nothing in between these two options, and employees who decide not to adhere to this principle are in breach.

ForYou-4U: This concept describes the four steps to create an engagement excellence experience for the customer or conversation partner by understanding, updating, undertaking and checking whether all was done up to their satisfaction. These four activities are related to the building blocks of engagement excellence as specified in the N(EX)3 model. See N(EX)3 model

Guiding principles: The MILL model can only work if both manager and employees stick to their respective guiding principles. The employees' principle is 'execute or escalate' or, in other words, either 'do what you say' or manage the expectations of your manager. The manager's principle is 'inspect what you expect' or, in other words, show care and control with regard to what you state to be important. These two guiding principles could be considered as the values within the MILL model.

Impact indicators: Measurable units that have a correlation with the results. Certain efforts are expected to create more or better results, and measuring these should be done by using impact indicators. If more calls will always result in more sales, the number of calls should be measured as an impact indicator. Impact is measured by comparing efforts (action goals) with outcome (result goals).

Inspect what you expect: The manager's guiding principle under the MILL model, which involves showing care for the employees by showing interest in their efforts and results. Everything that gets attention will grow, and this is applicable to management in terms of their engagement with employees.

Lagging indicators: Financial and other indicators that give a 'rear-mirror' view on what the outcome is so far. These indicators cannot be used to give guidance on actions or direction; they are more related to control and discovering whether actions taken so far have had impact as expected.

Learning cycle: This is the first blade of the MILL model. It explains the steps to follow to translate a learning experience into action improvement, and ensures that the grooming and development of employees will continue. The manager has to master this concept and apply the proper kind of care and control towards employees, to keep the cycle running.

Leading indicators: Measurable actions, resources or other requirements that are likely to contribute to results. These indicators are – unlike the lagging indicators – more forward-looking and can be used for planning and preparation. They should therefore get more attention than lagging indicators during meetings.

Lessons learned: These are new insights created by individual staff for learning and sharing with peers. They can be used for employees' personal growth and development, and therefore will also benefit the organisation. Lessons have been learned when the root cause of failure is clear and this knowledge can be used to make adjustments in the actions (action improvement) for a new and better attempt. The outcome of any action should be either a result or a lesson learned.

MILL model: MILL stands for Molenkamp Interactive Learning Leadership. The aim is to develop and groom staff while creating results for the organisation. The four 'blades' of the model explain what is expected from management and staff in terms of preparation and execution. The blades in the MILL model are connected by a set of key tools and guiding principles, and every blade can be broken into building blocks for a better understanding of how they work.

N(EX)3: This is related to the third blade of the MILL model – engagement excellence. N(EX)3 refers to the first letter of the four aspects that determine the quality of engagement for any customer or conversation partner, and therefore create, if executed well, engagement excellence. N(EX)3 is about (identifying) Needs, (managing), Expectations, (mastering) Execution and (verifying) Experience. These four steps together drive customer satisfaction, but also the relationships and cooperation among colleagues.

Net promoter score (NPS): This approach for scoring customer satisfaction is widely used to determine whether the customer would recommend the organisation. This approach can show trends for marketing departments or company boards, but will not indicate which aspects of engagement customers are happy with or complaining about. Therefore NPS cannot be used as input for action improvement. The ForYou/4U approach was developed as a much more useful alternative. See ForYou/4U

Outcome game: This approach challenges management to limit time spent exploring the past trying to find the culprit for failure, and instead to use these root causes and lessons learned to create commitment for improvement. Monitoring and accountability for the future should be put in place so that it is unlikely that the same issue will happen again. See also Blame game

Results: These are tangible outcomes that have direct benefit for the organisation. The outcome of any action performed under the commitment for action improvement is either a lesson learned (in the case of a full or partial failure) or results (in the case of achievements made in line with expectations). Both are considered to be successful outcomes, as they will both make the organisation stronger, either in performance or in competencies/knowledge.

Result board: The ideas for actions selected and committed to by employees will be captured on this centrally located board, which will also display the results expected by the end of week and a daily update on progress. The result board will be used to compare progress among peers in order to challenge and support each other, and will also be used as guidance for the end-of-week debrief in order to celebrate and learn as a team.

Result goals: These goals are jointly agreed between the manager and employees during the last step of the action improvement meeting. The intention is to aim high when setting the result goals in order to create some stretch and therefore a better focus and faster learning. Result goals are broken down to an individual level and captured both on the action card and result board. See also Action goals

Root cause: Understanding the reasons for success or failure may require more in-depth investigation to find the reason-behind-the-reason. Finding the root cause is done by repeating the 'why' question until it becomes clear where the problem/opportunity originates. The aim is to find something that can be acted upon or influenced by the employee ('... and what can you do about it ...')

Storytelling: Explaining, without evidence, why something did not happen and in general using a lot of time and words to get to the point. This kind of explanation is more about excuses and finger-pointing than exploring possible solutions and committing to actions. The opposite of storytelling is lessons learned followed by suggestions for action improvement. Storytelling should be discouraged as it will not contribute to the learning cycle.

Success: Defined under the MILL model as either results or lessons learned. Success is any outcome that relates to achieving a goal, or any outcome that has created new insights on what works or does not work. In both cases the employee and/or organisation will benefit, either immediately or in the short term. By using this definition, employees can be successful even if they do not bring results, as long as they know what action improvement will increase their impact.

APPENDICES

Checklist for management behaviour

COMMIT
Clarity brings closer

▶ It becomes easier to achieve goals and to be inspired if it is more clear to the employee how success exactly looks like

Empowerment for embedding

▶ In order to engage employees they should be enabled to determine HOW to reach the goal

DELIVER
Coaching is questioning

▶ To maximize development of strengths, the manager should minimize support and question to challenge.

Execute or Escalate

▶ The manager should challenge employees to give their best and manage expectations without blaming.

LEARN
Inspect your expectation

▶ To show care and make important what the manager believes is important, should be followed up.

Listening is learning

▶ Curiosity to find out what creates success and attention for every detail drives mastery for both manager and employee.

IMPROVE
Express your impression

▶ Crisp and clear and constructive feedback from the manager is the fuel for improvement and increased focus.

Stretching makes stronger

▶ Challenge yourself as a manager and the colleagues as there is always room for improvement until you retire

Checklist for staff behaviour

MORE

This is a matter of frequency. You are doing it but not often enough to really make it work, or it works well, so do it more. This is about changing habits from monthly to weekly or weekly to daily to increase focus and results. More consistency/ discipline is a strong driver for building success.

BETTER

This is a matter of quality. You can improve the efficiency of what you do anyway by improving the preparation, and practise doing better on the details of the execution. It could also be about better or more usage of tools and techniques. Further quality enhancing behaviours are self-assessment and asking for feedback.

DIFFERENT

This is a matter of creativity: you can make some big or small changes or try something else. This is about thinking out of the box, by looking from a different angle to your product, your industry or your customers. For example: how many ways to interact with collegues/customers do you have and did you try them all?

LESS

This is a matter of efficiency and focus: the goal is to work smarter, not harder so somewhere you should fine the time to do what is right by stopping or reducing everything else. Checking the added value of all that you do and checking whether you are the right person to do this work, could be an eye opener.

Action card   Action improvement (activity): ----------------------------

MANAGEMENT MASTER MIND

Date ----------   Employee: ------------

Action commitment(#) ------------   Result commitment (#): ----------

Planning	Activity scheduled	Activity realised	Successes (results or lessons learned)
Monday			
Tuesday			
Wednesday			
Thursday			
Friday			

Situation	Behaviour	Outcome	Learning

Result board Action improvement (activity): _____

Date _____ **Action commitment** _____ **Result commitment:** _____

Name employee	Action Commitment	Result Commitment	Mon Result	Tues Result	Wed Result	Thur Result	Fri Result	Total Result

Best performer _____ Runner up _____ Best lesson learned adopted _____

MANAGEMENT MASTER MIND

A WORD OF THANKS

I am grateful to all the people who supported me in writing this book. The belief and encouragement from my wife, Mira, was of course essential, and even my son, Ryan, had some good input. People who contributed a lot were Patrick van Dielen, Lesley Dawe (first edit) and especially Carolyn Jackson (Grammar Factory) who did a complete overhaul of the first version and contributed in many ways to the overall quality of the book. The internal art work was prepared by creative mastermind Tendai Machaka (Cornelius James)

Other people who supported me were my parents, Hans and Elly, who gave great feedback on several chapters and also on the title. Many more people also had good input and provided suggestions, and I also would like to thank Martin van Lonkhuijzen, Neal McIntrye, Bart Koster (CGA advies), Henk-Jan Molenkamp, Jacqui Pretty (Grammar Factory), Richard Chalk and, of course, supportive friends like Marcel Disberg, Jan Kruise, Francesco Marini Astrid Beuvink and Frans van Midde.

ABOUT THE AUTHOR

Arjan Molenkamp has almost twenty-five years management experience, of which the last seventeen have been in executive positions. He graduated in Economics and has an MBA from the Erasmus University of Rotterdam (Netherlands), and also completed various short-term programs at the Universities of Tel Aviv (Israel), Austin (USA), IMD (Switzerland), Harvard (USA), Oxford (UK) and Insead (France).

He has specialised in banking and occupied various executive roles, including Chief of Retail Banking, Head of Corporate Banking and Chief Operating Officer. After being appointed as Group Head for cultural and structural change programs in a large multinational, he expanded this experience by working with highly qualified change experts and consultancy firms like BCG. He is also a qualified practitioner in Neuro Linguistic Programming, and understands that impact of language and perception is on human behaviour. His work has allowed him to see how these learnings can be applied in the working environment.

The author has worked and lived in thirteen different places in eight different countries and has been exposed to many different cultures. He has spent the last ten years in Africa unleashing the potential of employees and customers in formerly state-owned banks and other enterprises. Success has many owners, but he made a large contribution to the nomination of Best Bank of the country for two of his employers. The MILL model principles described in this book have been developed, tested and improved in four different countries and on two continents since the idea of writing this book started some twelve years ago.